GRAVE
TIDINGS

Grave Tidings

An Anthology of Famous Last Words

PAUL BERRA

Biteback Publishing

First published in Great Britain in 2016 by
Biteback Publishing Ltd
Westminster Tower
3 Albert Embankment
London SE1 7SP
Copyright © Paul Berra 2016

ISBN 978-1-78590-102-7

10 9 8 7 6 5 4 3 2 1

A CIP catalogue record for this book is available from the British Library.

Set in Albertina by Adrian McLaughlin

Printed and bound in Great Britain by
CPI Group (UK) Ltd, Croydon CR0 4YY

For James Stephens (*il miglior fabbro*),
till death do us part.

'WHAT is the meaning of it, Watson?'
said Holmes, solemnly, as he laid down
the paper. 'What object is served by this
circle of misery and violence and fear? It
must be to some end, or else our universe
is ruled by chance, which is unthinkable.
But what end? There is the great standing
perennial problem to which human
reason is as far from an answer as ever.'

The Adventure of the Cardboard Box,
SIR ARTHUR CONAN DOYLE

CONTENTS

INTRODUCTION

In the midst of life, we are in death. Or, to paraphrase Jesus on the poor, the dead are always with us. They people our thoughts and memorials; they accumulate like dust behind locked doors and perch soberly atop bookshelves and mantelpieces.

They are, at the same time, intimately proximate and unfathomably distant. It is easy enough to join their ranks but to truly know them is not possible from our remove, despite the best guesses of priests, quacks, philosophers and the insane. At the heart of our relationship is a confounding and irresolvable ambiguity: we are them in the making.

But if sometimes they take up more space than we'd like, in other ways the dead can be very accommodating, allowing us to take tremendous liberties. Accordingly, we stand on their shoulders, walk in their shoes and hang on their every word.

Best of all, we make of them what we want, for they cannot be libelled and they never answer back.

Their parting words, in particular, hold an irresistible significance to us, spoken as they are in that liminal space between life and death. They seem to tell us something about ourselves, or, perhaps, something we would like to think about ourselves – that if we have no sway over death, we can at least control the way we leave this world. They teach us, rightly or wrongly, that death can be ameliorated by a sage word, its edge softened by a bluff joke. Often seeming to contain the accumulated wisdom of a lifetime's experience, they console and reassure us, amuse or even frighten us. Last words can be funny, reflective, scornful and inspirational, often revealing fortitude in the face of great suffering, or simple contempt for those remaining behind.

They can also be contentious, or improbable, ascribed afterwards to propagate some cultural or political ideal sacred to a later age. Or even simply to tell a good story.

Take the case of Julius Caesar. As he was being butchered on that March day in 44BC, did he truly wheel around to face his senatorial assassins and, recognising his friend Marcus Brutus among them, pronounce the most famous last words in history? Caesar's contemporaries have him dying silently, his cloak pulled over his head, yet William Shakespeare in Act III, Scene 1 of his eponymous play has Caesar address Brutus with, 'Et tu, Brute? Then fall, Caesar!'

The familiar dying words of the Roman proto-emperor are the product of a playwright's imagination, designed to inject pathos into a scene of horror and convey the hubris of an ambitious protagonist. And why not? The alternative – the screams of a dying man, the squelch of bowels involuntarily emptied on the forum floor and the frightened clucks of murderous politicians – lacks nuance by comparison.

In terms of plausibility, though, Shakespeare's version of Caesar's final words holds about the same amount of water as Kenneth Williams's in the 1964 comedy *Carry On Cleo*. As his assassin converges on him with daggers drawn, Williams's Caesar exclaims, 'Infamy! Infamy! They've all got it in for me!'

Death is, often, a messy business, and coherence in the face of it is a luxury rarely afforded. Caesar was stabbed twenty-three times according to Suetonius, so it is doubtful he had the time to project his collegial disappointment. The remains of another of Shakespeare's historical subjects, King Richard III, were found beneath a car park in Leicester in 2012. A very post post-mortem examination of his skeleton showing nine separate injuries to Richard's skull indicates that his last moments were quick and brutal: he was hacked to death on Bosworth Field, with barely time to cry for his mother let alone offer his king-dom in exchange for a horse.

In reality, last words can commonly be as insensible as those of Dutch Schulz, a New York gangster who was gunned down by Mafia rivals in the 1930s. The police attempted to question him as he lay in his hospital bed, but all Schulz could produce in his dying delirium was an admittedly compelling free-flowing babble, of which here is a taste:

> Please give me a shot. It is from the factory. Sure, that is a bad. Well, oh good ahead that happens for trying. I don't want harmony. I want harmony. Oh, mamma, mamma! Who give it to him? Who give it to him? Let me in the district fire-factory that he was nowhere near. It smoul-dered. No, no. There are only ten of us and there ten million fighting somewhere of you, so get your onions up and we will throw up the truce flag. Oh, please let me up. Please shift me. Police are here. Communistic … strike … baloney … honestly this is a habit I get; some-times I give it and sometimes I don't. Oh, I am all in. That settles it. Are you sure? Please let me get in and eat. Let him harass himself to you and then bother you. Please don't ask me to go there. I don't want to. I still

don't want him in the path. It is no use to stage a riot. The sidewalk was in trouble and the bears were in trouble and I broke it up. Please put me in that room. Please keep him in control. My gilt-edged stuff and those dirty rats have tuned in. Please, mother, don't tear, don't rip; that is something that shouldn't be spoken about. Please get me up, my friends. Please, look out. The shooting is a bit wild, and that kind of shooting saved a man's life. No payrolls. No wells. No coupons. That would be entirely out. Pardon me, I forgot I am plaintiff and not defendant. Look out. Look out for him. Please. He owed me money; he owes everyone money. Why can't he just pull out and give me control? Please, mother, you pick me up now. Please, you know me. No. Don't you scare me. My friends and I think I do a better job. Police are looking for you all over. Be instrumental in letting us know. They are Englishmen and they are a type I don't know who is best, they or us. Oh, sir, get the doll a roofing. You can play jacks and girls do that with a soft ball and do tricks with it. I take all events into consideration. No. No. And it is no. It is confused and it says no. A boy has never wept nor dashed a thousand Kim. Did you hear me?

The above was captured by a police stenographer, for

entirely practical reasons. Fascinatingly, however, the transcript later became an influence on writers of the Beat generation such as Robert Shea, Robert Anton Wilson and William S. Burroughs, who even used it as the bedrock of a surreal screenplay.

Sometimes, death gets in the way of a good story. The last words of the Mexican revolutionary Pancho Villa were: 'Don't let it end like this. Tell them I said something.' Villa, an early fan of the movies, lived his life as if in a film (he even signed a contract with a Hollywood studio who wanted to film his battles) and, like Shakespeare, was aware that good drama demands a killer pay-off line. So, as he lies bullet-ridden, victim of a roadside ambush, the media-savvy Villa purportedly urges an associate to think up the last words that he, in his death agonies, is not able to; grand words that will confer dignity on his life and cause. All fine so far. Except Villa's car was hit by a volley of forty bullets fired by seven gunmen. Villa himself was hit by nine bullets, four of which were dug out of his head, meaning he must have died instantly. His last words, words that have passed down through generations as accepted historical fact, were put in Villa's mouth at a later date, most likely taken from an obscure film version of the bandit's life made a decade after it ended. Truly attributed or not (that they are once-removed serves only to make the situation achingly post-modern), the words have become iconic in that they perfectly illustrate a tension in our love for famous last words. They interest us because they seem to complete a story, retrospectively validating a life that has been lived.

In that regard, they can also be redemptive. It was famously said of King Charles I of England, a truly execrable monarch who nevertheless put on a remarkable display of dignity and self-possession in his declamation at the axeman's block, that nothing so became him in life as the leaving of it. Though Charles's boldness pales in comparison to that of Major-General Thomas Harrison, a signatory to the king's death warrant, who, condemned to be hanged, drawn and quartered upon the Restoration, still managed to swing a punch at his executioner.

In the case of executions, last words are often used as an opportunity to set the story straight or to confer scorn on an enemy. Convicted killer Thomas J. Grasso used the occasion of his death by lethal injection to admonish the Oklahoma state prison system for not providing his requested last meal, claiming, 'I did not get my SpaghettiOs, I got spaghetti. I want the press to know this.'

So some of us die with great dignity, some of us die with a curse on our lips, and most of us die in complete anonymity; our last words unrecorded, our lives unregarded.

In this book are the last words of nearly 200 people, including lovers, killers, artists, traitors, spies, rulers, poets, dreamers and mystics, from times ancient and modern. Some are probably accurate, some most likely are not, and I confess I have by no means attempted to err on the side of caution in all cases, particularly where to do so would get in the way of telling a good story.

And therein lies the rub: amusing, exhorting, inspiring or chilling, behind all famous last words there is a story, and telling stories is what separates us from the dead – because stories are what we use to fend off the gathering night.

I

The Hedonists

Drinkers, gourmands, libertines
and the hopelessly entertaining

'CODEINE…
BOURBON.'

Tallulah Bankhead, d.1968

Tallulah Bankhead was, in her day, one of America's leading actresses on both stage and screen. Descended from United States senators, Bankhead's enormous talent is somewhat overshadowed to modern eyes by an appealing reputation as a libertine, and her famously liberal attitudes towards sex and drugs.

Probably bisexual (she referred to herself as 'ambisextrous'), Bankhead's outspoken libidinousness often got her into hot water, even garnering her a place on the Hays Committee's infamous blacklist, a government report presented to all Hollywood studios listing actors who were not be promoted to the public on grounds of moral turpitude.

Bankhead suffered terribly from addictions to both alcohol and drugs. Unable to sleep without the aid of handfuls of prescription drugs, she reputedly had to be tied to her bed at night to prevent her unconscious body from shovelling nearby pills into her mouth. As she lay dying in St Luke's Hospital, Manhattan, on 12 December 1968, she was asked if she needed anything. Her last coherent words, above, were in response.

'I'VE HAD EIGHTEEN STRAIGHT WHISKEYS. I THINK THAT'S THE RECORD.'

Dylan Thomas, d.1953

Born in Swansea at the start of the First World War, Thomas was the most significant Welsh poet of the twentieth century. Writing in English, he is celebrated for poems such as 'Do not go gentle into that good night', 'Fern Hill' and 'Love in the Asylum', as well as for the radio play _Under Milk Wood_. Famously patronising London's bohemian drinking district of Fitzrovia in the '40s and '50s, Thomas developed a parallel reputation as a hell-raiser and alcoholic, which was exacerbated by a complex, often destructive relationship with his wife Caitlin Macnamara, to whom he was serially unfaithful.

Unable to live by writing alone, Thomas supplemented his lifestyle with broadcasting, and with poetry tours of the United States. It was on one such trip, in November 1953, that Thomas finally came to grief. Already unwell,

Thomas spent most of the 3rd drinking in his room at New York's Chelsea Hotel.

Later he went out to the White Horse pub in Greenwich Village, boasting upon his return that he had drunk eighteen whiskeys in a row. At some point over the next two days, Thomas slipped into a coma from which he would not emerge. He died at St Vincent's Hospital on 9 November 1953.

'I SHOULD NEVER HAVE SWITCHED FROM SCOTCH TO MARTINIS.'

Humphrey Bogart, d.1957

Charismatic, tough and versatile, Humphrey DeForest Bogart was the quintessential Hollywood male lead of the 1940s, becoming a screen legend for his roles in films including *Casablanca*, *The Maltese Falcon* and *The African Queen*, as well as for his portrayal of hardboiled detective Philip Marlowe in *The Big Sleep*.

'Bogie' was a founder member of the Rat Pack, essentially a drinking club for Hollywood stars, which included Frank Sinatra, Dean Martin, Sammy Davis Jr, Peter Lawford and Joey Bishop. A lifetime of heavy drinking and smoking took its toll on Bogart when, in 1956, he discovered he had cancer of the oesophagus. True to his on-screen tough-guy persona, Bogart kept the illness to himself until it was too developed to be successfully treated. He passed away on 14 January 1957, allegedly blaming a change in drinks for his misfortune.

This seems to be an incorrect attribution, however, and his true last words were more likely, and appropriately, to have been, 'Good-bye, Kid. Hurry back,' spoken to his young wife, Lauren Bacall, as she briefly left his bedside. She returned to find him comatose and he died soon after.

'ONE LAST DRINK, PLEASE.'

———

Jack Daniel, d.1911

Suspiciously apt, these are said to be final words of businessman and founder of the Jack Daniel's Tennessee Whiskey Distillery, as he lay dying of blood poisoning in October 1911.

Daniel was born in Lynchburg, Tennessee, probably around 1849, the descendant of Welsh and Scottish settlers from the eighteenth century. He went on to found his famous whiskey (America uses the Irish spelling, as opposed to the more universal Scots 'whisky') distillery in about 1875. It is said that Daniel often had trouble remembering the combination to the large safe in his office. One morning he kicked it in frustration, injuring the toes on his foot. Infection soon spread and he died on 10 October.

'I'VE HAD A HELL OF A LOT OF FUN, AND I'VE ENJOYED EVERY MINUTE OF IT.'

———

Errol Flynn, d.1959

Born in Hobart, Tasmania with bankable good looks and an athletic physique, Errol Leslie Thomson Flynn was trouble from the word go. Thrown out of every school he attended, and in constant strife with both the law and jealous husbands, he eventually jumped ship for England, then America, where his natural talents were put to good effect in the movies.

Discovered by Warner Brothers, he became the star of swashbucklers and adventure films, including *Captain Blood*, *They Died with Their Boots On* and *The Adventures of Robin Hood*. Off screen, he unstintingly indulged his passions for drinking, fighting and sex, and was later involved in a personally disastrous trial for statutory rape (for which he was acquitted, though not without the expression 'In like Flynn' having been coined in dubious honour of his apparently relaxed attitude towards sexual consent).

Over time, his hedonistic lifestyle, and attendant law-suits, caught up with him, and he died dissolute and ruined at the age of fifty, in the arms of his fifteen-year-old lover.

'I WISH I HAD DRUNK MORE CHAMPAGNE.'

———

John Maynard Keynes, d.1946

Without doubt the most influential economist of the twentieth century – the ubiquitous epithet 'Keynesian' having been coined in his honour and applied to everything from Franklin Roosevelt's New Deal to the founding of the World Bank and International Monetary Fund – Maynard Keynes was, however, emphatically no stuffed shirt.

In fact, he only became an economist by accident, applying for the job at his old Cambridge college despite lacking any background in or experience of the subject. Keynes was also bisexual and spent much of the Edwardian era secretly conducting affairs with young men, often actors. A prominent member of the famously free-thinking Bloomsbury set, his last words reflect his remarkably enlightened attitude towards life.

'YOU MIGHT MAKE THAT A DOUBLE!'

Neville Heath, d.1946

Neville Heath was a charming man, blessed with dashing looks, who combined a career in His Majesty's armed forces with that of a thief, forger, deserter, rapist and murderer. He was tried for the murder of Margery Gardner, whose mutilated body was found tied to a hotel-room bed in Notting Hill, though he is known also to have killed Doreen Marshall, the naked remains of whom were discovered a month later on a Bournemouth beach.

Found guilty and sentenced to hang, Heath's execution was carried out by England's last official hangman, Albert Pierrepoint, on 16 October 1946 at London's Pentonville prison.

As was the custom, minutes prior to the execution the prison governor offered the condemned man a last glass of whisky, to which Heath gave the above reply.

'DIE? I SHOULD SAY NOT, DEAR FELLOW. NO BARRYMORE WOULD ALLOW SUCH A CONVENTIONAL THING TO HAPPEN TO HIM.'

John Barrymore, d.1942

In the 1920s, at the height of his powers, John Barrymore was celebrated as the greatest Shakespearian actor in the world. Twenty years later, he was completely washed up, his career fatally compromised by his passion for drink.

The scion of the famous Drew and Barrymore acting families, Barrymore easily made the transition from the silent movies to the talkies, and revolutionised the way Shakespeare was performed on both stage and screen. As he got older, however, his hectic private life (he got through four wives and innumerable lovers) began to eclipse his art. Alcoholism affected his ability to memorise lines and limited the roles he was offered. Eventually, he was reduced to playing parodies of his own drunkenness. Despite his last words, Barrymore did indeed die on 29 May 1942, as a result of cirrhosis of the liver.

'IT WOULD BE HARD IF TWO
SUCH FRIENDS SHOULD PART
WITHOUT AT LEAST
ONE SWEET KISS.'

———

Turlough O'Carolan, d.1738

Turlough O'Carolan was a blind harpist, composer and singer who achieved great fame in Ireland in the early eighteenth century. Dying, he called for one last glass of whiskey with the above, quite reasonable, justification.

'BLESS YOU, SISTER, MAY ALL YOUR SONS BE BISHOPS.'

Brendan Behan, d.1964

B orn into a nationalist family in Dublin in 1923, Brendan Behan is regarded as one of Ireland's greatest writers, albeit one whose talents were eroded by success and alcohol. When the IRA launched a bombing campaign in England on the eve of the Second World War, Behan was trained in explosives and sent to participate. Arrested immediately upon his arrival in Liverpool, he spent three years in a borstal, where a decent library set him to learning his future trade.

The autobiographical *Borstal Boy* is based upon his experiences at this time, but it was his 1954 play *The Quare Fellow* which would cement Behan's reputation as one of the finest writers of his generation. To his detriment, perhaps, Behan soon learned, following a series of drunken public appearances, that it paid to play the inebriated Irishman, famously describing himself as a 'drinker with a writing problem'.

Quickly becoming a darling to the media, Behan soon found fame hard to deal with and played his chosen role a little too well. He died in Meath Hospital on 20 March 1964 at the tragically young age of forty-one, and his coffin was escorted by an IRA guard of honour.

'I KNEW IT. I KNEW IT. BORN IN A HOTEL ROOM – AND GOD DAMN IT – DIED IN A HOTEL ROOM!'

———

Eugene O'Neill, d.1953

The writer of that quintessentially American play, *Long Day's Journey into Night*, did indeed die in a hotel room. He passed away on 27 November 1953 in room 401 of the Sheraton Hotel, Boston. The building would later become a student dormitory for Boston University, with successive occupants perpetuating the myth that O'Neill's gloomy ghost still walks the halls. And where was he born? Also in a hotel – The Barrett House, at Broadway and 43rd Street, New York, now a part of Times Square.

'THEN LET'S FORGET ABOUT IT AND PLAY HIGH FIVE.'

———

Buffalo Bill Cody, d.1917

The career of William Frederick 'Buffalo Bill' Cody runs parallel with the story of the American Old West. He rode for the Pony Express as a child, fought in the Civil War on the side of the Union, was decorated for his work as a scout in the Indian Wars, and did more than any man to popularise the image of the Wild West by staging massive shows depicting scenes from frontier and cowboy history, and touring them across the world. His last words were in response to his doctor telling him he hadn't long to live.

'GOOD! A WOMAN THAT CAN FART IS NOT DEAD!'

The Comtesse de Vercellis, d.1728

Thérèse de Vercellis was an eighteenth-century French noblewoman whose chief claim on history is that she took mercy on the sixteen-year-old future philosopher Jean-Jacques Rousseau, employing the young runaway as a footman. The unfortunate lady was dying with breast cancer. As her illness progressed, she turned Rousseau into a secretary to deal with her correspondence.

He records her death in his own autobiography, *Confessions*, thus:

> She only kept her bed the two last days, and continued to converse quietly with everybody to the end. At last, speaking no more, and already in the agonies of death, she broke wind loudly. 'Good!' she said, turning around. 'A woman that can fart is not dead!' These were the last words she uttered.

'THERE'S FUN
IN THE AIR.'

Maurice Chevalier, d.1972

So spoke Chevalier to the priest who arrived to take his confession, before quietly slipping into unconsciousness. Maurice Auguste Chevalier began life as an acrobat before his career was cut short by a terrible accident. Trying his luck at acting and singing, his ambitions were again interrupted, this time by the outbreak of the First World War, in which the unlucky Chevalier was again wounded, before being taken prisoner by the Germans.

After his release, the pieces finally began falling into place for Chevalier when he travelled to Hollywood. There his heavy French accent, melodic tones and beguiling charm secured him roles in films such as *Gigi*, for which he sang the signature tunes 'Thank Heaven for Little Girls' and 'I Remember It Well'.

'I AM IMPLORING YOU – BURN ALL THE INDECENT POEMS AND DRAWINGS.'

———

Aubrey Beardsley, d.1898

Aubrey Beardsley was a Victorian illustrator whose humorous, erotic and iconic drawings lampooned the age he lived in and provided inspiration for the nascent Modernism of the twentieth century. He found fame as the art director for the infamous, highly bohemian *Yellow Book*, though he was soon ubiquitous in his employment, lending sumptuous illustrations to Malory's *Le Morte d'Arthur* and to Oscar Wilde's *Salome*. A late-life conversion to Catholicism appears to have occasioned this deathbed request from Beardsley to his publisher, Leonard Smithers. Fortunately, Smithers ignored it.

'HOW IMPERIOUS ONE IS
WHEN ONE NO LONGER
HAS TIME TO BE POLITE.'

———

Jeanne-Louise-Henriette de Campan, d.1822

Beginning life as a lady-in-waiting to the doomed Marie Antoinette, Madame Henriette de Campan nevertheless survived the French Revolution and flourished as a teacher under the reign of Napoleon. This was her response to a friend's criticism of her sharp treatment of a maid.

'LET NOT POOR NELLY STARVE.'

———

King Charles II, d.1685

Charles II has gone down in the history books as the very definition of the libertine. Frankly, given the times he lived in, who could blame him? His father was executed by his own subjects, and Charles himself was surrounded by men who would gladly have seen the same done to him.

The period following the Restoration of the monarchy was a dangerous time for a new king, with religious and political tensions running extremely high. Accordingly, Charles did what any sensible young man in his position would have done; kept his cards close to his chest, played it dumb and went to the theatre, a pastime banned for decades under the Puritans and only recently re-established by Charles himself. It was at the theatre that Charles found several of his numerous mistresses. In fact, Charles II never produced a legitimate heir, though he could boast at least twelve children with his mistresses, most of whom were expensively ennobled, much to the taxpayers' chagrin.

Upon his deathbed, he imported his brother James to take care of his mistresses, including the actress Nell Gwyn, who by this time was suffering from the syphilis that would kill her three years later. She had accumulated significant debts and was no doubt glad of the £1,500-a-year pension James subsequently arranged for her.

'DAMMIT! DON'T YOU DARE ASK GOD TO HELP ME.'

Joan Crawford, d.1977

So said the actress to her housekeeper who, annoyingly, began to pray aloud as Crawford lay dying. An extremely independent woman, Crawford's career was no accident, but the result of hard graft and good fortune. Born into poverty, Crawford got her break in the movies, becoming the highest-paid female film star of the 1930s and achieving acclaim and success for movies such as *Mildred Pierce* (for which she won an Oscar) and *What Ever Happened to Baby Jane?*, in which she starred alongside Bette Davis. Davis famously said of her bitter rival, 'She's slept with every male star at MGM except Lassie.'

'You see! This is how you die.'

Coco Chanel, d.1971

The work of fashion designer Gabrielle 'Coco' Chanel has had a profound influence on the way women dress even today. The inventor of the little black dress, the garçon haircut and, of course, Chanel No.5 perfume was, during her lifetime, the embodiment of style, elegance and self-confidence. Dying as she lived, these were the final words she spoke to her maid and doctor before she passed away in her Hotel Ritz bedroom in Paris on 10 January 1971.

'THANK GOD. I'M TIRED OF BEING THE FUNNIEST PERSON IN THE ROOM.'

————

Del Close, d.1999

American actor, writer and humorist Del Close died surrounded by friends in Chicago's Illinois Masonic Hospital on 4 March 1999. Expressing the regret he never got to play Hamlet, Close allegedly bequeathed his skull to Chicago's Goodman Theatre after his death so that at least he would get to play Yorick.

'OH, YOU YOUNG PEOPLE ACT LIKE OLD MEN. YOU HAVE NO FUN.'

―――――

Josephine Baker, d.1975

Dancer, singer, actress, civil rights activist, the irrepressible Josephine Baker was born into poverty in St Louis, Missouri, in 1906. Unwilling to concede to the many obstacles placed in her way, Baker became the first black female performer to star in her own movie, and toured her sensational erotic cabaret around the world.

She famously performed her 'Danse Sauvage' dressed only in a skirt made of bananas, shocking even the regulars at Paris's notorious Folies Bergère. Eventually settling in France, where she would later be awarded the Croix de guerre and Légion d'honneur for her work with the wartime resistance, the above words were allegedly spoken as the 68-year-old Baker tried unsuccessfully to seduce a much younger man just hours before her death.

'THAT WAS THE BEST ICE-CREAM SODA I EVER TASTED.'

Lou Costello, d.1959

One half of the most successful American comedy double act of all time, Lou Costello died of a heart attack in Los Angeles on 3 March 1959, a few days short of his fifty-third birthday. His last words express satisfaction at a particularly good strawberry ice-cream soda shared with his wife and manager just prior to his demise.

'I THINK I COULD EAT ONE OF BELLAMY'S MEAT PIES.'

William Pitt the Younger, d.1806

William Pitt the Younger (to distinguish him from his father, who also served in the role) remains Britain's youngest ever Prime Minister, having first taken the office at the age of twenty-four, and he held the position twice. His premierships oversaw the country's response to the French Revolution and the Napoleonic Wars, and Pitt himself is regarded as having revived the Tory Party and paved the way for British expansionism that would lead to empire.

His health suffered under the strain of public life and his various conditions were exacerbated by a fondness for port wine that was unwisely encouraged by his doctor. In his febrile waning hours, Pitt, who had hitherto been unable to eat, suddenly evinced an appetite for a meat pie. A messenger was duly sent, but by the time Bellamy arrived with his wares, the Prime Minister had died.

'I JUST WISH I HAD TIME FOR ONE MORE BOWL OF CHILI.'

Kit Carson, d.1868

Frontiersman, scout, trapper, soldier, Indian agent and authentic legend of the Old West, Kit Carson's name is synonymous with many of the pivotal events in America's westward expansion, including the Civil War, the Indian Wars and the conflict with Mexico, where he developed his appreciation of chili, the frontiersman's ideal repast, easy as it was to transport and prepare.

'GET MY SWAN COSTUME READY.'

————

Anna Pavlova, d.1931

Anna Pavlova was the most famous prima ballerina of her day. Renowned for her dedication to her art, when Pavlova contracted pleurisy and was given the choice of a career-ending operation or death, she chose the latter. She died in the small hours of 23 January 1931 attended by her maid and doctor, to whom she left the instruction to bury her in the costume of the Dying Swan, her most celebrated role. The next time the ballet was performed, a single spotlight illuminated Pavlova's vacant place on the stage in honour of the great ballerina.

'WHY SHOULD I TALK TO YOU? I'VE JUST BEEN TALKING TO YOUR BOSS.'

Wilson Mizner, d.1933

———

Few had careers as varied as Wilson Mizner. At various times a playwright, petty thief, raconteur, business-man, boxing impresario, restaurateur and gambling den operator, he is best known today for the wise words and witticisms he bequeathed to the English language (for example, Mizner first extolled the wisdom 'Be nice to peo-ple on the way up because you'll meet the same people on the way down'). He even spent a time as a Hollywood scriptwriter, an experience he likened to taking 'a trip through a sewer in a glass-bottomed boat'. His dying words, typically, were a riposte to an attendant priest urging him to unburden his soul.

'I AM IN A DUEL TO DEATH WITH THIS WALLPAPER. ONE OF US HAS TO GO.'

Oscar Wilde, d.1900

Oscar Wilde recovered neither physically nor psychologically from his two years' hard labour at Reading jail. Following his release, he fled to France in disgrace, nursing a ruptured ear drum. As he wandered around Europe, an infection took hold in his ear which later developed into cerebral meningitis. Fatally ill, Wilde remarked to his friends, 'I am dying beyond my means. I can't even afford to die.' He dwindled and died in his room in the Hôtel d'Alsace on 30 November 1900, his final words making clear his distaste for its décor.

'O LORD, FORGIVE THE ERRATA!'

———

Andrew Bradford, d.1742

Andrew Bradford was a Philadelphia printer and proto-press baron who opened the city's first newspaper, the *American Weekly Mercury*, in 1719. Professional to the last, on his deathbed he issued this earnest appeal to God to excuse him for any typographical errors that may have appeared in the paper during his stewardship.

'DON'T LET THEM SHUT THE THEATRES FOR ME.'

King Oscar II of Sweden, d.1907

Himself a writer and composer of some talent, Oscar II was also a considerable patron of the performing arts in his native Sweden. Fittingly, his final request was that his civil servants eschew the traditional closure of the nation's theatres upon the death of a monarch.

'NO. I AM CURIOUS TO SEE WHAT
HAPPENS IN THE NEXT WORLD TO
ONE WHO DIES UNSHRIVEN.'

———

Pietro Perugino, d.1523

Pietro Vannucci, nicknamed Perugino because he hailed
from Perugia in Umbria, was an Italian Renaissance
painter and one of the period's earliest adopters of oils.
He counted Raphael among his pupils and Michelangelo
among his enemies (he once took the latter to court for
defamation and lost, ruining himself financially).

In a time when faith was not optional, Perugino was
controversially rumoured to be harbouring doubts
about the immortality of the soul. True or not, at the end
of his life, when the priest came to hear Perugino's confession and give absolution for his sins, the painter chose
the risky option.

'BRING DOWN THE CURTAIN: THE FARCE IS ENDED.'

———

François Rabelais, d.1553

Rabelais is widely considered to be one of the most influential French writers of the Renaissance. His *Gargantua and Pantagruel* became the bedrock for a Western literary tradition of employing coarse humour and bold caricature.

Indeed, so robust was his satire that the sixteenth-century priest, scholar and humanist found himself condemned by the religious authorities so that, throughout his life, he was forced to rely on the patronage of great men in order to avoid prosecution for heresy.

Upon his death, he is said to have spoken the above words to his friend, leaving also a one-line will, 'I owe much; I have nothing; the rest I leave to the poor.'

'CURTAIN! FAST MUSIC! LIGHT!
READY FOR THE LAST FINALE! GREAT!
THE SHOW LOOKS GOOD,
THE SHOW LOOKS GOOD.'

———

Florenz Ziegfeld, d.1932

Flo Ziegfeld was a celebrated Broadway impresario, best known for his extraordinary review shows which blended outrageous sets with the presence of beautiful and scantily clad young women, modelled upon the Folies Bergère of Paris.

He died of pleurisy in a Los Angeles hospital room. Slipping in and out of consciousness, he believed in his delirium that he was directing one last theatrical spectacular.

'DID I PLAY MY ROLE WELL? IF SO THEN APPLAUSE, BECAUSE THE COMEDY IS FINISHED.'

Augustus, d.14

Augustus was born in the Republic of Rome and died its first, and greatest, emperor, having presided over a period of unprecedented peace in the Roman world and the expansion of Rome's frontiers from Spain to Africa.

As a consequence of observing the sticky end of his adopted father Julius Caesar – stabbed to death in the Senate for brashly parading the trappings of power – throughout his own reign Augustus was careful to maintain the illusion of being Rome's servant, and never to be seen openly pulling its strings. His last words refer to the relentless performance required to pull off this momentous masquerade.

'YOU CAN KEEP THE THINGS OF
BRONZE AND STONE AND GIVE ME
ONE MAN TO REMEMBER ME JUST
ONCE A YEAR.'

———

Damon Runyon, d.1946

Damon Runyon's short stories evoke a prohibition-era New York of gangsters and their molls, most in evidence in *Guys and Dolls*, his enduringly popular work. Dying of throat cancer, his appealing final words were passed in a note to his close friend Walter Winchell.

'WHERE IS
MY CLOCK?'

———

Salvador Dalí, d.1989

The last words of Salvador Dalí are as enigmatic and, frankly, weird as this artist's life, which, with a passion for excess and a flare for publicity, sometimes appeared a continuation of his surreal art. The motif of the melting clock occurs throughout his paintings and it is said the artist took his inspiration from watching a Camembert cheese deliquesce in the sun.

'NOW I SHALL GO TO SLEEP. GOODNIGHT.'

———

Lord Byron, d.1824

George Gordon Noel, Baron Byron, was the apogee of the Romantic poet. Famously described by a contemporary as 'mad, bad and dangerous to know', Byron gained a notoriety for his flamboyance and scandalous love life, and he allegedly fathered a child with his half-sister.

It was this, mounting debts and a passion for adventure that eventually made him leave England and travel widely across Europe. He contracted fever in Missolonghi fighting against the Ottomans in the Greek War of Independence, uttering the above rather sweet words before he passed away.

'GOD BLESS, GOD DAMN!'

———

James Thurber, d.1961

Thurber is celebrated as one of America's greatest humorists and cartoonists, a career that is particularly remarkable since he was almost completely blind due to a childhood accident in which his brother shot him in the eye with an arrow whilst playing a game of William Tell. His cartoons and short pieces celebrated everyday American life and appeared regularly in the *New Yorker* magazine.

'I DESIRE TO GO TO HELL AND NOT
TO HEAVEN. IN THE FORMER I SHALL
ENJOY THE COMPANY OF POPES,
KINGS AND PRINCES, WHILST IN
THE LATTER ARE ONLY BEGGARS,
MONKS AND APOSTLES.'

———

Niccolò Machiavelli, d.1527

The term 'Machiavellian' is today used to describe a shrewd political operator, determined to succeed and unburdened by moral constraints in the doing so. It is based on Machiavelli's best-known work, *The Prince*, a guide to often unscrupulous Renaissance statecraft which has resonated down the ages and seems to find disconcerting parallels in today's political hierarchies. In fact, far from the devilish figure associated with his book, Machiavelli was simply a proponent of what we would later call realpolitik, as this well-reasoned deathbed response to his priest might suggest.

2

Parting Shots

Saints, spies, kings, killers, heroes
and the irremediably unlucky

'THIS SIDE IS ROASTED ENOUGH, TYRANT, TURN ME OVER!'

St Lawrence, d.258

The fantastically improbable last words of St Lawrence, who, according to legend, was martyred for his beliefs by being roasted alive on a man-sized gridiron. With gruesome if predictable irony, he subsequently passed into the ranks of the holy as patron saint of cooks and chefs.

'IT DOESN'T HURT, PAETUS!'

Arria Major, d.42

A rria was the wife of the unfortunate Roman senator Caecina Paetus, who, ordered to commit suicide by the emperor Caligula, lost his nerve at the last moment. For encouragement, Arria seized her husband's dagger and plunged it into her own breast, before handing it back to Paetus with the above words.

'TELL THEM I DIED GAME.'

Fred Lowry, d.1863

Lowry was a bushranger, horse thief and outlaw who terrorised his native New South Wales and was responsible for countless robberies as well as the deaths of several men. Shot in the neck as police tried to apprehend him, his last words were spoken to the trooper who comforted him.

'TAKE A STEP FORWARD, LADS. IT WILL BE EASIER THAT WAY.'

Erskine Childers, d.1922

Robert Erskine Childers is best remembered as the author of the Edwardian adventure novel *The Riddle of the Sands*. A staunch supporter of British imperialism who fought in the Boer War and World War One, he later recanted and became an ardent Irish nationalist.

Arrested during Ireland's civil war, he was tried and executed for carrying an illegal weapon. Before his execution, he shook hands with each member of the firing squad in turn and, remarkably, made his sixteen-year-old son promise to repeat the reconciliatory gesture after the shooting.

'DEATH IS NOTHING, NOR LIFE
EITHER, FOR THAT MATTER.
TO DIE, TO SLEEP, TO PASS
INTO NOTHINGNESS, WHAT
DOES IT MATTER? EVERYTHING
IS AN ILLUSION.'

———

Mata Hari, d.1917

Margaretha Geertruida Zelle (she would later take the stage name Mata Hari, meaning 'eye of the morning') was a Dutch-born exotic dancer who was much admired in Paris just before the First World War. When war broke out, she became a spy for the French intelligence services, using her status as a citizen of neutral Holland with dancing engagements across Europe as cover to cross borders without suspicion. However, she was arrested in her Paris hotel room in February 1917 and accused of being a double agent for the Germans, which papers discovered half a century later would confirm.

She was tried and found guilty, and her sentence of death by firing squad was carried out on 15 October 1917.

Very few female spies were executed in World War One, and the impossibly glamorous Mata Hari certainly captured the public imagination. According to an eye-witness, she presented herself for death adorned in a dress trimmed with fur, a large felt hat and lavender kid gloves, refusing to be blindfolded and smiling to the last.

'I AM STARTING TO BELIEVE YOU ARE NOT INTENDING TO COUNT ME AMONG YOUR FRIENDS!'

———

Pedro Muñoz Seca, d.1936

The Spanish Civil War claimed the lives of many thousands of its brightest citizens on both sides of the royalist/republican divide. Among them was comic playwright Pedro Muñoz Seca, several of whose dramas were highly critical of the Second Spanish Republic. Muñoz Seca was arrested and sent before the firing squad. His last words to them were typical of his essentially comic perspective.

'I PRAY YOU TO BEAR ME WITNESS THAT I MEET MY FATE LIKE A BRAVE MAN.'

John André, d.1780

Major John André fought for the British Army as its head of secret intelligence during the American Revolutionary War. He befriended and plotted with the American general Benedict Arnold to surrender the key fort at West Point to the British but was captured, tried and sentenced to death by the American Continental Army. Eyewitnesses record that André went to his death at the hands of the hangman with great fortitude, even though he had expressly requested to die by firing squad and was severely dismayed to see the hanging cart trundled out.

'ARE YOU SURE IT'S SAFE?'

William Palmer, d.1856

———

Facing his fate with rather less fortitude than Major André, and somewhat missing the point to boot, William Palmer, the so-called 'prince of poisoners', famously displayed concern as to the robustness of the gallows whilst stepping out onto its platform to be hanged for murder.

'I HAVE JUST HAD TO TELL YOUR
MOTHER THAT I SHALL BE DEAD
IN A QUARTER OF AN HOUR. TO
DIE BY THE HAND OF ONE'S OWN
PEOPLE IS HARD. BUT THE HOUSE
IS SURROUNDED AND HITLER
IS CHARGING ME WITH HIGH
TREASON. IN VIEW OF MY SERVICES
IN AFRICA I AM TO HAVE THE
CHANCE OF DYING BY POISON.
THE TWO GENERALS HAVE BROUGHT
IT WITH THEM. IT'S FATAL IN THREE
SECONDS. IF I ACCEPT, NONE OF THE
USUAL STEPS WILL BE TAKEN AGAINST
MY FAMILY, THAT IS, AGAINST YOU.
THEY WILL ALSO LEAVE MY
STAFF ALONE.'

Field Marshal Erwin Rommel, d.1944

Rommel was one of Nazi Germany's most popular and highly decorated generals, who earned the

nickname the 'Desert Fox' for a series of extraordinary victories against the Allies in north Africa. Later in the war, having become disenchanted with Hitler's governance, Rommel was involved in a failed plot to assassinate the German Führer.

Because Rommel was fêted as a national hero, Hitler did not want to publicly execute him and instead offered him the chance to commit suicide in exchange for not persecuting Rommel's family after his death. Rommel accepted Hitler's offer and in his last recorded words explained his choice and its consequences to his teenaged son, as his house was quietly surrounded by a detachment of SS guards. Shortly thereafter, Rommel climbed into a staff car and was driven away by two officers to ingest cyanide. He was buried with full military honours.

'LET IT BE KNOWN THAT HOMOSEXUALS ARE NOT COWARDS.'

Willem Arondeus, d.1943

D utch artist and writer Willem Arondeus was openly homosexual before the Nazi invasion of the Netherlands in 1942, and quickly recognised, with the eye of someone himself not unused to persecution, that the Nazis' registering of Dutch Jews was not for innocent purposes. As well as secretly publishing literature calling for resistance, Arondeus joined an underground group forging false documents to allow Jews to escape Holland. When the Germans began exposing the documents as fakes by comparing them with originals in the local register, Arondeus led a group that bombed Amsterdam's Public Records Office to destroy the evidence.

Soon afterwards, however, he was betrayed and arrested, then tried and sentenced to death by firing squad. Arondeus's last words were a thrilling act of resistance against the regime, and he would posthumously receive honours from both the Netherlands and Israel for his bravery and actions.

'PARDON ME, SIR, I DID NOT DO IT ON PURPOSE.'

Marie Antoinette, d.1793

Marie Antoinette was perhaps the most famous victim of 'la Grande Terreur', the wave of revolutionary violence that swept away tens of thousands of France's most eminent personages.

As the glamorous wife of the ineffectual King Louis XVI, she was unfortunate to have been associated in the public mind with the ills besetting France in the late eighteenth century. The country was deep in debt, yet the queen spent lavishly, her profligacy earning her the nickname 'Madame Déficit'. To compound her poor public image, when told that French peasants were starving with no bread to eat she was alleged to have remarked rather callously, 'Let them eat cake!' – a further indication of the ruling family's remoteness from its subjects.

Despite this, for a time she proved a far more capable ruler than her feckless husband. However, regardless of her prowess, the royal family was taken into custody by the revolutionary government and she followed the king to the guillotine on 16 October 1793, tripping over the executioner's foot on the way to the scaffold and courteously apologising for the offence.

During the height of the terror, guillotine executions became a gruesome form of mass entertainment, with both crowd and victim playing their part. Killings became a daily event and people would flock to the Place de la Révolution like spectators to a football match today. Indeed, programmes listing the day's victims were sold by vendors, and miniature guillotines were sold as children's toys or vegetable dicers. 'Tricoteuses' would sit knitting on the scaffold, and those about to be beheaded would sometimes dance or perform little skits on its steps to amuse their audience, often delivering humorous or defiant imprecations.

One such victim was Georges Jacques Danton, an architect of the revolution who later found himself caught up in its terror. His final words to the executioner were the vainglorious entreaty, 'Don't forget to show my head to the people. It's well worth seeing.'

'DO NOT KEEP ME
IN SUSPENSE!'

Henri de Talleyrand-Périgord, d.1626

Henri de Talleyrand-Périgord, Comte de Chalais, was an aristocrat who fell victim to an earlier French regime, that of Cardinal Richelieu. His last words, spoken on the scaffold, were an earnest petition to his executioner. Unfortunately, the unskilled axeman then took over thirty blows to sever the luckless Talleyrand's head.

'This is a sharp medicine, but a sure remedy for all illness and misery.'

Sir Walter Raleigh, d.1618

France was not the only country with a penchant for beheading its leading subjects. When Raleigh went to the block on exaggerated political charges designed to placate the Spanish (whose treasure ships Raleigh had plundered imperiously on behalf of his own king), the elderly adventurer was first allowed to check the keenness of the axe blade and remarked that it would at least provide a cure for the agues plaguing him.

His head was afterwards embalmed and presented to his widow as a grisly memento. Nonetheless, she kept it with her in a velvet bag until her own death nearly thirty years later.

'Prithee, let me feel the axe. I feel it is not sharp enough.'

James, Duke of Monmouth, d.1685

James Scott, 1st Duke of Monmouth, was the eldest illegitimate son of Charles II, who haplessly led an attempted rebellion against his father's successor, his own uncle, James II. The rebellion failed and Monmouth was captured and executed for treason on London's Tower Hill.

His final plea was for the infamous axeman Jack Ketch to exercise accuracy in his death blow and to use a keen blade. Monmouth would have been better advised to keep his words to himself, however. The entreaty served only to put Ketch off his stroke, leading him to deliver multiple botched blows before finally drawing a knife to detach Monmouth's head.

'THE EXECUTIONER IS, I BELIEVE, VERY EXPERT, AND MY NECK IS VERY SLENDER.'

———

Anne Boleyn, d.1536

Anne Boleyn was the second wife of King Henry VIII and the mother of the future Queen Elizabeth I. Condemned to die on dubious charges of adultery, incest and high treason, Anne's chief crime seems to have been her failure to produce a male heir for her husband. Usually a job for the axe, Henry at least showed his wife the small mercy of importing a professional swordsman from France to carry out the dreadful deed.

'THIS HATH NOT OFFENDED THE KING.'

Thomas More, d.1535

———

Lawyer, philosopher and statesman, Thomas More was Henry VIII's Lord High Chancellor and closest counsellor until he too fell foul of the king's capricious nature. More objected to England's separation from the Catholic Church, and his refusal to acknowledge Henry as Supreme Head of the Church of England sealed his fate. Mounting the scaffold to be decapitated, he proudly announced himself 'the king's good servant, but God's first', before shifting his beard to one side to avoid the axeman's blade, giving the above justification for his action.

'JESUS! JESUS! JESUS!'

Joan of Arc, d.1431

J eanne d'Arc, the 'Maid of Orleans', was a peasant girl who received visions of saints and angels telling her to help the French king reclaim his lands from the English during the Hundred Years' War. She persuaded Charles VII to give her a chance and was sent at the head of the French Army to relieve the besieged city of Orleans. She did so admirably, winning several more improbable victories before she was finally captured by the Burgundians at Compiègne. They promptly sold her to the English, who tried her for heresy. She was burned at the stake in Rouen on 30 May 1431 and herself became a saint five centuries later.

'WHAT AN ARTIST DIES IN ME!'

Emperor Nero, d.68

Brutal, ineffectual and vindictive, Nero was the last of the emperors descended from Augustus, and among the worst in Rome's long history of terrible rulers. In twelve mostly turbulent years, Nero managed to foment revolution in the provinces, burn Rome to the ground, kill his own mother, have one wife executed and personally kick another to death, poison his brother and most capable advisors and alienate the Senate – who eventually declared him an enemy of the people.

Amusingly, though inaccurately, Nero thought himself a great singer and composer on the lyre and, to the horror of the fiercely hierarchical Roman upper classes, tastelessly performed several times in public. Worse, on occasion he entered singing competitions in Rome and Greece and, unsurprisingly for a notorious ruler with a reputation for grudge-bearing, won them too. Cornered and forced to commit suicide with the help of his slaves, Nero's self-pitying last words are emblematic of his excessive and deluded existence.

'STRIKE HERE! SMITE MY WOMB!'

———

Agrippina the Younger, d.59

Possessed of ruthless ambition and born with an over-weening sense of entitlement, Agrippina was the great-granddaughter of Augustus, the mother of Nero and the wife of the emperor Claudius, who she poisoned to make way for her son.

Having engineered Nero's path to power, Agrippina sought to realise her ambitions by ruling through him. Nero soon tired of her interference, however, and at first sidelined her before deciding to do away with his mother altogether.

He invited her aboard a yacht that was ingeniously designed to fall apart at sea. The boat duly collapsed but Agrippina managed to escape and swim safely to shore. The frustrated Nero then opted for a less showy, more direct method, simply sending men with swords to his mother's villa.

Seeing the soldiers arrive, and realising she had backed

the wrong horse in Nero, Agrippina ordered her killers to stab first at the belly that had carried her wretched son in pregnancy.

'AH, WELL, I SUPPOSE IT HAS COME TO THIS ... SUCH IS LIFE.'

Ned Kelly, d.1880

Ned Kelly is one of Australia's greatest folk heroes, a latter-day Robin Hood figure. Kelly was the son of Irish convicts and belonged to a marginalised class that faced constant persecution from the authorities. Eventually, after a number of convictions for horse theft and other crimes, Kelly and his brothers took to the bush where they became fully fledged bushrangers, robbing banks, shooting policemen and generally waging war on upholders of the law.

Kelly and his gang made their last stand in a hotel in the small town of Glenrowan, Victoria. Surrounded by police, Kelly attempted to escape in a suit of armour he'd had made the previous year. The armour covered his body but left his extremities exposed, so his pursuers were able to shoot him in the legs and apprehend him. Tried and found guilty of murder, Kelly uttered the above words before he was hanged on 11 November 1880 at Melbourne jail.

'WHO'S THERE?'

Billy the Kid, d.1881

With eight kills to his name, William H. Bonney, alias Billy the Kid, is the best known of the Old West's outlaw gunslingers, acquiring fame in his own lifetime as America's newspapers carried reports of his deeds to an urban readership hungry for thrills.

He was eventually apprehended and killed by Sheriff Pat Garrett in Fort Sumner, New Mexico. Garrett found out where the Kid was staying and waited for him in his darkened chamber. Entering the room, Billy called out in Spanish, 'Who's there?' Recognising his voice, Garret then shot him dead.

'THAT PICTURE IS AWFUL DUSTY.'

———

Jesse James, d.1882

At a loose end after fighting on the losing side in the American Civil War, Jesse and his brother Frank James formed and led the infamous James–Younger Gang, and proceeded to rob banks, stagecoaches and trains across the American Midwest for nearly sixteen years.

With a reward of $5,000 placed on his head by the Governor of Missouri, it was only a matter of time before Jesse James was betrayed. This he was by Robert Ford, a member of his own gang, who shot James in the back of the head as he reached up to clean a dirty picture.

Ford never received his reward, however. He was run out of town by the governor and forced into hiding. Eventually his actions caught up with him and he was brutally murdered by an irate fan of the popular outlaw he had killed.

Jesse James himself was buried with a gravestone that read, '*In Loving Memory of my Beloved Son, Murdered by a Traitor and Coward Whose Name is not Worthy to Appear Here.*'

'WE ARE THE FIRST VICTIMS OF AMERICAN FASCISM!'

Ethel Rosenberg, d.1953

Ethel and Julius Rosenberg, the infamous atomic spies, were the first civilians in American history to be executed for espionage. As the leader of a spy ring centred on the Manhattan Project – America's nuclear weapons research and development facility – Julius Rosenberg smuggled top-secret information to the Russians that enabled them to accelerate the production of their own nuclear bomb.

The spies were caught when the FBI decoded important Soviet cables. Refusing to confess to their misdemeanours, the Rosenbergs were sentenced to death and executed in the electric chair at sundown on 19 June 1953.

Evidence appearing subsequently casts doubt on Ethel Rosenberg's involvement in her husband's spying, strongly suggesting she was victim to a frightful miscarriage of justice.

'GOOD PEOPLE ARE ALWAYS SO SURE THEY'RE RIGHT.'

Barbara Graham, d.1955

Barbara Graham was sentenced to death in the gas chamber for her part in the murder of an elderly woman, Mabel Monohan, in her home in Burbank, California. Graham allegedly gained Monohan's confidence to get access to her house, then let in her two accomplices. After killing Monohan, the gang left empty-handed, ironically missing thousands of dollars' worth of stashed jewellery in their search of the house. They were soon apprehended and Graham, the only woman in their number, was demonised in the press as 'Bloody Babs'. Her trial defence fell apart when she tried to bribe a fellow inmate to provide her with an alibi for the night of the murder and she was sentenced and transferred to death row at San Quentin state prison to await execution.

In truth, regardless of her guilt, Graham never really stood a chance. The unwanted product of a teen pregnancy, raised by strangers and the California penal reform system, Graham was a beautiful vagrant who eked out a living working as a prostitute and a petty criminal.

Her final words are chilling because of the implication that she saw herself as a being from a separate race to 'good' people.

'HURRAH FOR ANARCHY! THIS IS THE HAPPIEST MOMENT OF MY LIFE.'

———

George Engel, d.1887

Georgeorge Engel was a German socialist and Chicago toy store owner who was accused, along with seven other men, of conspiring to let off a bomb in that city's Haymarket Square during a workers' rights protest. The device went off, killing seven policemen, and although Engel was not present at the time, he was later arrested, tried and sentenced to be hanged. Several of his co-defendants were shown clemency and it seems likely Engel himself would have been pardoned had he not written to Illinois Governor Richard Oglesby demanding that clemency not be considered in his own case.

'FOR THE SAKE OF DECENCY, GENTLEMEN, DON'T HANG ME HIGH.'

Mary Blandy, d.1752

Mary Blandy poisoned her father with arsenic when he disapproved of the suitor she had set her heart upon. Her case was notorious in mid-eighteenth-century England partly because of her sex, and partly because she came from a well-to-do background and was unusually well-educated for a murderer. As she mounted the gallows, her final words were an appeal to the officiating parties to protect her modesty in death, and prevent men in the crowd from looking up her skirts as her body swung on the gibbet.

'I CURSE YOU, CORWIN, AND ALL OF SALEM!'

———

Giles Corey, d.1692

New England's most notorious witch trials took place in 1692, when a group of young girls in Salem Village, Massachusetts, claimed to be possessed by the devil and denounced local women as witches. Salem landowner Giles Corey was caught up in the ensuing wave of hysteria when he dared to speak out against the girls, questioning their sincerity.

Subsequently accused of witchcraft himself, Corey refused to validate the charge by pleading either guilty or innocent to it. Unable to try him without a plea, contemporary law allowed his judges to submit Corey to pressing, an obscure torture involving a board being laid on the victim's naked body and a series of increasingly heavy stones being placed atop the board.

Designed to elicit a confession, Corey instead offered only defiance, three times demanding more weight be laid upon him. It took him two days to die a horrible death. His last words were an imprecation on Sheriff George Corwin, the official who had subjected him to it, and the town of Salem that had fallen for the girls' claims.

'Long live Soviet sport!'

Nikolai Trusevich, d.1943

On 9 August 1942 a football match took place in Nazi-occupied Ukraine that has passed into sporting legend. On one side was FC Start, a team made up of workers from a bread factory who had played for Ukraine's most successful team, Dynamo Kiev, before the German invasion. Their opposition in Kiev's Zenit stadium was Flakelf, composed of footballers from the German Army. This was a rematch. Three days earlier, FC Start had demolished the Germans 5–1, and the Reichskommissar had ordered the second game as a chance for the German team, now strengthened by the inclusion of elite players from across the Nazi-occupied territories, to gain revenge.

Indeed, the pitch was lined by SS guards and snarling police dogs, and before the game the Ukrainian players were visited by a Gestapo officer who warned them to deliberately lose or to face the consequences. The game itself was a dirty one. The Germans fouled the Ukrainians with impunity, even assaulting and concussing goalkeeper Trusevich, scoring two goals whilst he lay on the grass bleeding. Despite their opponents' aggression and the implied threat to their own lives, the Ukrainians went on to win the match 5–3, completing the Nazis' humiliation. The regime kept its word, however, and nine days later the Gestapo arrived at Bakery Number 3 and removed four members of FC Start for questioning, Trusevich among them.

Trusevich and his colleagues were sent to the nearby Syrets concentration camp where they were shot six months later. Stood at the edge of the infamous Babi Yar ravine, already containing the bodies of 33,000 Jews murdered in a single day at the beginning of the Nazi occupation, Trusevich stared down the soldiers detailed to kill him and shouted, 'Long live Soviet sport!'

At least, that was the official post-war Soviet account of Trusevich's demise. In reality, eye-witness reports suppressed at the time and NKVD archives released following the fall of the Soviet Union leave contemporary historians doubting the validity of the entire 'death match' legend. Spectators at the game report no SS guards or atmosphere of intimidation, and photographs taken after the match appear to show Ukrainian and German players in relaxed conversation, even drinking vodka together. Moreover, match reports from contemporary

German-censored Ukrainian newspapers reveal teams from both sides of the occupation regularly played each other, with the Germans losing as often as they won. Trusevich and his teammates were indeed arrested, sent to the camp and murdered. However, it now seems likely they were victims of a petty grudge, wrongly denounced to the occupation authorities as saboteurs and spies by the manager of a rival Ukrainian football team.

The goalkeeper's final words and the death match legend is probably the creation of Soviet propagandists after the war, keen to counter a prevailing notion that the people of Ukraine had not resisted the occupation with sufficient vigour.

Whatever the truth of his final words, Nikolai Trusevich, goalkeeper for FC Start, was executed on 24 February 1943 in Syrets concentration camp on the edge of Kiev, consumed, like so many others, by the unfeeling machine of war.

'SHOOT STRAIGHT, YOU BASTARDS! DON'T MAKE A MESS OF IT!'

———

Breaker Morant, d.1902

Harry 'Breaker' Morant was an Australian bush drover and soldier who commanded a British irregular unit, the Bushveldt Carbineers, during the Second Boer War in South Africa. Although he otherwise served with distinction, he was enraged by the Afrikaners' killing and mutilation of his friend, in retaliation for which he ordered the unjudicial execution of Boer prisoners, then sanctioned the murder of a German missionary who threatened to expose his crime.

Court-martialled and sent before a firing squad, his last words, along with an impression he was the victim of political machinations, have made him an Australian folk hero almost in the mould of Ned Kelly.

'MY MOTHER DID IT.'

———

Arnold Rothstein, d.1928

Racketeer, gangster and kingpin of New York's Jewish mob in the early twentieth century, Arnold 'The Brain' Rothstein is credited with having elevated crime to the level of corporate enterprise, even allegedly fixing the 1919 Baseball World Series. Shot and mortally wounded by a rival over a gambling debt, Rothstein refused to name his assailant, instead using his dying breath to mock the inquiring police.

'I COULD SHOOT BETTER!'

Hannie Schaft, d.1945

Johanna 'Hannie' Schaft was a member of the Dutch resistance to the Nazi occupation during World War Two. She began her clandestine career by helping people in hiding from the Germans, supplying them with false identification cards and food coupons, though she graduated to openly defying the occupiers and attacking collaborators.

Hannie was arrested at a military checkpoint in March 1945 and, although the Nazis had by now agreed with the Dutch authorities to stop all executions, she was assigned for death. Shot at close range by a two-man firing squad, she was initially wounded and delivered the above retort, before the Germans finished their job. Hannie Schaft was buried in a shallow grave among the sand dunes at coastal Bloemendaal. It was only three weeks before the end of the war, and she was just twenty-four years old.

'YOU SONS OF BITCHES. GIVE MY LOVE TO MOTHER.'

———

Francis Crowley, d.1932

Francis 'Two Gun' Crowley was an Irish-American gangster who went on a three-month crime spree in 1931 that shocked and thrilled the nation. Crowley's rampage culminated in at least one murder, numerous woundings, and a two-hour stand off against 300 armed members of the NYPD in an apartment building on New York's Upper West Side, before he was finally captured. He was sent to the electric chair on 21 January 1932 and departed with these defiant words. He was just nineteen years of age.

'I WISH THE WHOLE HUMAN RACE HAD ONE NECK AND I HAD MY HANDS ROUND IT.'

Carl Panzram, d.1930

Thief, arsonist, rapist and serial killer, Carl Panzram was a very bad man indeed. Brutalised by youthful experiences in children's homes and prisons, Panzram later went on an eight-year orgy of death that, according to his own memoirs, resulted in the killings of twenty-one people, though this is not completely verifiable.

He was finally sentenced to hang for bludgeoning a prison foreman to death in 1929. He spat the above words in the face of his executioner as he put the noose around Panzram's neck, before exhorting him to 'hurry it up, you Hoosier bastard! I could kill a dozen men while you're screwing around!'

'YES –
A BULLETPROOF VEST!'

James W. Rodgers, d.1960

S entenced to death for murder by the state of Utah, James Rodgers was the last prisoner to be executed by firing squad before the US Supreme Court put a stop to the practice. Asked if he had any last requests, he famously asked for the above.

'How about this for a headline for tomorrow's paper? "French Fries!"'

James French, d.1966

James D. French was already serving a life sentence for the killing of a motorist whilst hitchhiking when he decided to kill his cellmate in order to compel the state of Oklahoma to execute him. He went to the electric chair on 10 August 1966. One suspects he had been working on his famous last line for some time.

'WELL, GENTLEMEN, YOU ARE ABOUT TO SEE A BAKED APPEL!'

———

George Appel, d.1928

Though perhaps not as long as George Appel, who was electrocuted in 1928 for the murder of a New York City police officer.

'YOU GOT ME.'

John Dillinger, d.1934

Along with Bonnie and Clyde, John Dillinger was the most notorious of America's Depression-era gangsters. Robbing at least twelve banks, raiding four police stations and escaping custody twice, he met his end in a shootout with federal agents at a Chicago theatre in 1934. Fatally wounded, the dying Dillinger exhibited a late talent for stating the obvious.

'IF ANY OF YOU HAVE A MESSAGE FOR THE DEVIL, GIVE IT TO ME, FOR I AM ABOUT TO MEET HIM!'

———

Lavinia Fisher, d.1820

Lavinia Fisher is reputedly the first female serial killer in the history of the United States. Along with her husband John, Fisher ran an inn, the Six Mile Wayfarer House, just outside Charleston, South Carolina, where legend has it they together robbed and murdered dozens of unsuspecting travellers.

The facts have been somewhat obscured by the more romantic legend, but it seems accurate at least to conclude the pair were members of a gang of highwaymen. Both were found guilty of highway robbery and sentenced to hang.

John Fisher protested his innocence to the end but the brazen Lavinia reportedly appeared at the gallows in her wedding dress, offering to carry the crowd's tidings to the devil.

'I'LL BE IN HELL BEFORE YOU START BREAKFAST! LET HER RIP!'

Tom 'Black Jack' Ketchum, d.1901

Thomas E. Ketchum was a Texan cowboy who later began a life of crime with the outlaw Hole-in-the-Wall Gang. He was apprehended when an ill-conceived bid to single-handedly rob a train predictably went wrong, leaving Ketchum wounded by the trackside.

Sentenced to hang in Union County, New Mexico, he was (and remains) the first man ever to receive capital punishment in the district. Accordingly, the inexperienced officiators left the rope too long and the portly Ketchum was decapitated.

'HURRY IT UP! I WANT TO BE IN HELL IN TIME FOR DINNER.'

———

Edward H. Rulloff, d.1871

Clearly, the closer one gets to death the hungrier one becomes. Edward Rulloff was a noted philologist with a sideline in murder. Condemned for the killing of a store clerk, Rulloff's was the last public hanging ever to take place in New York City. His mortal remains were donated to medical science, whereupon his brain was discovered to be abnormally large. At 102 cubic inches it is the second largest brain on record and can be seen today at the psychology department of Cornell University.

'TELL THE BOYS
I'M COMING HOME.'

Wilbur Underhill, d.1934

Wilbur Underhill was one of four Missouri brothers, all of whom became career criminals, though Wilbur was by some measure the worst. Specialising in bank robbery, burglary and murder, Underhill was nicknamed 'Mad Dog' and the 'Tri-State Terror', becoming the most wanted man in Depression-era Oklahoma.

Celebrating his honeymoon, a relaxed Underhill was surrounded by armed federal agents at a cottage in Shawnee, Oklahoma. After a brief shootout, Underhill was hit five times but managed to flee the scene in his underwear, breaking into a nearby furniture store where he passed out on a bed. Dying in hospital a few days later, Underhill's last words were directed to the brothers who had pre-deceased him.

3

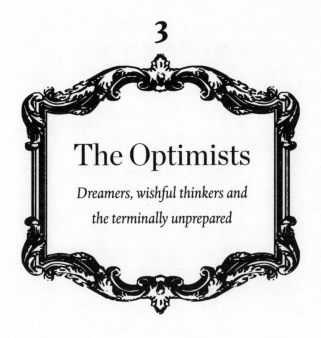

The Optimists

*Dreamers, wishful thinkers and
the terminally unprepared*

'I'VE NEVER FELT BETTER.'

Douglas Fairbanks, d.1939

During the silent movie era, Douglas Fairbanks was the undisputed 'King of Hollywood', starring as pirates and adventurers in countless blockbusters. With the coming of the talkies, however, Fairbanks's career went into swift decline.

Finding that he couldn't jump around like he did in his pre-sound roles and with theatre receipts taking a knock in the Depression, he lost heart and simply retired. His last words were spoken following a mild heart attack on 12 December 1939. He died later that day.

'THEY COULDN'T HIT AN ELEPHANT AT THIS DISTANCE.'

———

General John Sedgwick, d.1864

John Sedgwick was not the luckiest of soldiers. Fighting for the Union in the American Civil War, he was wounded heading up a disastrous charge at the Battle of Antietam, leading to his missing the centrepiece Battle of Fredericksburg.

When he returned to full health, he led his corps late to the Battle of Gettysburg, missing all the action. His famous last words were spoken at the Battle of Spotsylvania Court House a year later, upon which utterance the hapless Sedgwick was felled by a Confederate sharpshooter's bullet.

'DIE, MY DEAR DOCTOR? THAT'S THE LAST THING I SHALL DO.'

Viscount Palmerston, d.1865

Henry John Temple, 3rd Viscount Palmerston, spent so long at the heart of power in Great Britain that when he died it surprised even him. Beginning as a Tory, then turning into a Whig, before leading the newly formed Liberals into power, Palmerston (intriguingly nicknamed 'The Mongoose') spent six decades in government and remains the last, and oldest, Prime Minister to die in office.

'I STILL LIVE!'

———

Caligula, d.41

The third emperor of Rome, Caligula regularly tops polls as the worst, with only perhaps Nero and Commodus running him close in terms of cruelty, lasciviousness and sheer wet-lipped lunacy. After a promising start – no difficult task given the low bar set by his predecessor Tiberius – the new emperor succumbed to an illness from which he emerged with a sensational bloodlust.

Caligula killed or exiled all those close to him, then by all accounts set to work on everyone else. He once ordered the spectators at a public games thrown to the lions simply because he was bored. He is said to have raped brides in front of their grooms on their wedding nights and to have committed incest with his own sisters at public banquets. Such was his disdain for Rome's officials (a group he purged bloodily in an excess a later age might deem worthy of Joseph Stalin), he planned to enrol his favourite horse, Incitatus, in the Senate.

Where his grandfather Augustus sought to disguise his authority, Caligula did whatever he could to advance the pomp and priority of his office, and whatever depravities he might unleash upon the ruling classes, the people of Rome, at least, adored him. Until the money ran out, of course, then he was on his own, and he had built up a list of enemies so vast it was only a matter of time before one of the many conspiracies plotted against him paid off.

He was killed by members of the Senate and of his own Praetorian Guard as he conversed with a group of actors during some games. His last words, spoken in relieved surprise following the attack, were a little hasty. Hearing them, his killers simply returned to finish the job.

'THIS IS NOT
THE END OF ME.'

———

Henry Campbell-Bannerman, d.1908

So spoke British Prime Minister Henry Campbell-Bannerman on 22 April 1908, but it was, and he promptly expired, to this day the only Prime Minister ever to die inside 10 Downing Street, only nineteen days after his resignation. In fact, Campbell-Bannerman was first to do several things: the first man to be called Prime Minister (before him the official name of his post was First Lord of the Treasury), and the first man to hold the positions of Prime Minister and Father of the House of Commons simultaneously.

Campbell-Bannerman famously remarked, 'Personally, I am an immense believer in bed, in constantly keeping horizontal: the heart and everything else goes slower, and the whole system is refreshed.' And in bed is, fittingly, where he ended his days.

'LIFT ME UP THAT I MAY DIE STANDING, NOT LYING DOWN LIKE A COW.'

———

Siward the Dane, d.1055

'In bed' is emphatically not where this eleventh-century Danish enforcer wanted to be, especially as his end drew near. Unfortunately for Siward, who ruled an area in the north of England roughly corresponding to modern-day Yorkshire, he was struck down by dysentery. Flabbergasted that he could survive so many fearful battles yet succumb to mere sickness, Siward at least had the consolation of being clothed by servants in in his armour, helmet and shield when he died.

'IT IS NOTHING...
IT IS NOTHING...'

Archduke Franz Ferdinand
of Austria-Hungary, d.1914

The assassination of Franz Ferdinand in Sarajevo in 1914 set off a chain of events that dragged every power in Europe domino-like into a conflict that would last more than four years and claim the lives of at least sixteen million people.

What began as a sightseeing tour around the capital of the Austro-Hungarian province of Bosnia and Herzegovina was interrupted by bombs thrown by Serbian separatists. Outraged by the violence, Franz Ferdinand insisted on being taken to the hospital to visit the wounded. His driver, however, confused at the change of itinerary, got the archduke's open-top car jammed across a narrow street.

Armed, and disbelieving his luck, Serb nationalist Gavrilo Princip was sitting at a café across the street. He rose calmly, walked over to the car, shot first the archduke's wife, then Franz Ferdinand himself. Asked by an attendant if he was in much pain, the archduke repeated the above line several times then passed away.

'THE CAR
SEEMS OK...'

Ayrton Senna, d.1994

The death of Ayrton Senna at the 1994 San Marino Grand Prix shook the world of motor racing to its roots. The Brazilian ace, already winner of three Formula One World Championships for the McLaren team, was driving for Williams when his car left the track at 191 mph on lap seven and ran straight into a concrete retainer wall.

Although he was airlifted to Bologna's Maggiore hospital, he had sustained terrible head injuries and was pronounced dead within hours of his arrival. Widely regarded as one of the greatest racing drivers of all time, his death was mourned by fans of the sport who speculate what he might have gone on to achieve, and by the people of his native Brazil, three million of whom lined the streets of his hometown, São Paulo, for his funeral.

'DON'T WORRY…
IT'S NOT LOADED…'

Terry Kath, d.1978

Terry Kath was a founding member of the US rock band Chicago and one of the most distinctive and influential guitarists of the 1960s and '70s, with no less a figure than Jimi Hendrix calling him his favourite guitar player. Latterly, Kath was plagued by drug and alcohol problems, dependencies that mixed dangerously with a fondness for hand guns, which he regularly carried around with him.

On 23 January 1978, at a house party in Los Angeles, Kath put an unloaded .38 revolver to his head and pulled the trigger several times. Warned to be careful, Kath offered the above reassurance before returning to the game, this time using a semi-automatic 9mm pistol. Unfortunately, the gun was not empty and the next time he pulled the trigger he shot himself in the temple, dying instantly.

'SHOOT, WALTER, IN THE NAME OF HEAVEN, SHOOT!'

King William II, d.1100

William Rufus was the third son of William the Conqueror, from whom he inherited the kingdom of England. Hunting in the New Forest on 2 August 1100, William sited a stag and urged his companion, Walter Tirel, to shoot it before it could flee.

Tirel accordingly loosed his arrow, but it bizarrely managed to bypass the stag altogether, instead coming to rest in William's lung, leaving the king regretting his words.

'GO AWAY.
I'M ALL RIGHT.'

___

H. G. Wells, d.1946

Herbert George Wells, the so-called 'Father of Science Fiction', introduced the world to such nightmares as *The Invisible Man, The Island of Doctor Moreau* and, most famously, *The War of the Worlds*, which, when adapted for radio by Orson Welles in 1938, caused widespread panic across America as millions assumed they were listening to coverage of an actual Martian attack.

Towards the end of his life, and having witnessed two world wars, Wells became increasingly depressed at what he considered the hopeless future of mankind. He died of a suspected heart attack on 13 August 1946 at his London home, after sending concerned friends away with the above reassurance.

'AM I DYING
OR IS THIS
MY BIRTHDAY?'

Nancy Astor, d.1964

Nancy Witcher Langhorne Astor, Viscountess Astor, was the first woman to sit in the House of Commons as a Member of Parliament in the United Kingdom, remaining there for over twenty-five years. Witty, strident and often fearsome, she was outspoken in defence of women's rights, frequently rubbing up against the other denizens of what had previously been an all-boys' club.

She once famously remarked to Winston Churchill, 'If you were my husband, I'd poison your tea,' to which Churchill replied, 'Madam, if you were my wife, I'd drink it!' In later years her popularity waned as her views began to seem old-fashioned. Before the war, she campaigned for appeasement with Nazi Germany and appeared, in her correspondence, to hold anti-Semitic views.

In 1946, she was forced to step down, and with retirement came a gradual and lonely decline. Her last words were spoken as she came out of a sleep during her final illness to find herself surrounded by her children. She died on 2 May 1964 at Grimsthorpe Castle in Lincolnshire.

'I SHALL HEAR
IN HEAVEN!'

Ludwig van Beethoven, d.1827

Composer and pianist Ludwig van Beethoven, widely considered the greatest composer of all time, is remarkable not only because he created some of the finest and most famous music known to humanity, but also because he was either completely deaf or going deaf as he did so.

Beethoven struggled to conceal his failing hearing for a number of years, whilst continuing to compose at an astonishing rate. During his middle, or 'Heroic', period, as his hearing loss became acute, he nonetheless produced an opera, six symphonies, four solo concerti, five string quartets, six string sonatas, seven piano sonatas, five sets of piano variations, four overtures, four trios, two sextets and seventy-two songs – including the incomparable 'Moonlight Sonata'.

During his final years, now completely deaf, he composed his finest music of all, including the sublime Ninth

Symphony, with its towering choral finale 'Ode to Joy'. Beethoven died on 26 March 1827, at the age of fifty-six. Given he composed some of the most beautiful music ever heard, yet never got to hear a note of it himself, one can appreciate the wistfulness of his famous last words.

'GOD WILL PARDON ME – IT IS HIS PROFESSION.'

Heinrich Heine, d.1856

Spoken in confident riposte to a friend's suggestion he seek absolution, the dying poet Heinrich Heine had been confined to his 'Mattress grave' for nearly eight years, the result of what was assumed at the time to be venereal disease, though modern experts speculate it could have been multiple sclerosis.

The one-time heir to a wealthy Rhineland Jewish family (he later converted to Christianity as Jews were not allowed to practise law in the German states), Heine's fame grew with his poetic stature. His brilliant verse was infused with his radical political views, however, and he inevitably found himself banned by the state authorities, then exiled altogether. He died penniless in Paris, as all great poets ought.

'EVERYBODY HAS GOT TO DIE,
BUT I HAVE ALWAYS BELIEVED
AN EXCEPTION WOULD BE MADE
IN MY CASE. WHAT NOW?'

William Saroyan, d.1981

The son of Armenian immigrants fleeing the Ottoman Empire to California, his family's experiences went on to underpin many of William Saroyan's short stories and plays, including the collection *My Name is Aram*. Winning and rejecting the Pulitzer Prize for drama, Saroyan's work celebrates the joys of life in spite of hunger, poverty and instability. This celebration of existence appears to be reflected in the title of another of his famous works, *The Human Comedy*, and also perhaps in the poignant breeziness of his final words.

'NOLI TIMERE.'

———

Seamus Heaney, d.2013

Gathered to observe a requiem mass in Dublin following the death of the great Irish poet, mourners heard Seamus Heaney's son Michael describe how his father's powerful last words were shown in a text to his wife. The text read, in Latin, *'Noli timere'*, which simply translates as 'Do not be afraid'.

'ALL MY POSSESSIONS FOR A MOMENT OF TIME.'

Queen Elizabeth I, d.1603

That Elizabeth Tudor made it through her childhood, let alone to the throne of England, is a triumph over the improbable. The daughter of Henry VIII and Anne Boleyn, her birth was a bitter disappointment to her father who was waiting for a male heir, making Elizabeth a living symbol of her mother's apparent inability to produce one (a failing for which the latter would pay with her life and whose famous last words we have already seen on p. 66). Disinherited, declared illegitimate and imprisoned at the age of only two, Elizabeth's lonely youth was spent being shuttlecocked around the great houses of England.

Kept at arm's length during the upheavals following Henry's death, she was nevertheless continuously impugned or imprisoned on some unlikely charge or other during the brief reign of her brother Edward VI and the bloody one of Mary I, and nearly lost her head on more than one occasion. This sequence of being done to rather than doing ended when, there being no one else alive, Elizabeth acceded to the throne of England at the age of twenty-five, and proved to be one of the greatest rulers in the country's history.

Inheriting a nation torn by religious and economic strife, during her forty-four years on the throne Elizabeth returned the country to Protestantism, settled its political turmoil, fought off the Spanish and oversaw the unprecedented expansion of England's influence, chiefly in the New World. She is generally believed to have died of blood poisoning caused by the daily application of white face make-up made of lead and vinegar.

'I'M LOOKING FOR A LOOPHOLE.'

W. C. Fields, d.1946

As the great American comedian, writer and actor was dying in a Pasadena sanatorium, a friend came across him reading the Bible and asked the avowed atheist what he was doing. Fields's reply, above, was typical of his quick-fire wit. It is popularly, though sadly inaccurately, believed that the inscription on Fields's grave reads, 'I'd rather be in Philadelphia.'

'I BELIEVE WE MUST ADJOURN THE MEETING TO SOME OTHER PLACE.'

Adam Smith, d.1790

Adam Smith, father of political economy and founder of free-market economic thinking (that commerce should not be regulated and that freedom of trade produces prosperity for all), remains one of the most influential philosophers of the last 500 years. His book *An Inquiry into the Nature and Causes of the Wealth of Nations* remains the blueprint for economic theory in the twenty-first century, and his assurance that mutual self-interest is the only way to secure peace and plenty is the basis for the global economic system in which we all live, namely capitalism. Holding one last philosophical talking shop on his deathbed, and sensing his end was near, Smith dismissed his colleagues with the above words.

'I AM NOT THE LEAST
AFRAID TO DIE.'

———

Charles Darwin, d.1882

If Adam Smith changed the way we interact, Charles Darwin revolutionised the way humans think about ourselves altogether. The scientist and naturalist's magnum opus, *On the Origin of Species*, established the scientific theory of natural selection: the notion that all species descend through time from common ancestors, arbitrarily navigating by way of multiple series of evolutionary modifications.

Although the book proved highly controversial on its publication, Darwin's times were broadly ready for his theory, and it was received as the victory of science over religion. Darwin, however, described himself as an agnostic and remained open to the idea of God as an originating principle, though with design taken out of his or her hands by the application of evolution.

Regardless of the damage his own theory had done to the biblical version of history, with its attendant concept of life after death, Darwin at the end of his own life announced himself unconcerned about confronting his own mortality.

'I'LL FINALLY GET TO SEE MARILYN.'

Joe DiMaggio, d.1999

Joe DiMaggio played his entire career for the New York Yankees, to this day holding a record for a 56-game hitting streak, and being named an All-Star in each of his thirteen seasons (as well as helping the Yankees to ten American League pennants and nine World Series championships), making him one of the greatest centre-fielders ever to have graced the sport of baseball.

DiMaggio and movie star Marilyn Monroe married in January 1954, and divorced 274 days later. Their relationship improved dramatically thereafter, however, and DiMaggio was a constant source of strength in Monroe's turbulent life – supporting her when her marriage to Arthur Miller fell apart, checking her in and out of sanitaria when her mental health collapsed and trying to ameliorate what he saw as the malign influences of certain individuals she became involved with in her later years.

DiMaggio had assumed they would eventually remarry, but Marilyn's death in August 1964 put paid to that dream. The devastated DiMaggio claimed her body and arranged her funeral, sending six red roses to her grave three times a week for the next twenty years. DiMaggio never remarried and refused to talk publicly about their time together, though he died with her name on his lips.

'THAT'S THE FISH OF MY DREAMS.'

Dan Dodds, d.2011

Proving you don't have to be famous to speak famous last words, retired contractor Dan Dodds at least died doing what he loved: fishing. He spent twenty minutes in a battle to the death with a Chinook salmon, eventually landing a fine 28lb specimen. The elated Dodds told a nearby fisherman, 'That's the fish of my dreams,' before suffering a fatal heart attack and pitching face forward into the water.

'SOUTHERLY GALES, SQUALLS, LEE RAIL UNDER WATER, WET BUNKS, HARD TACK, BULLY BEEF, WISH YOU WERE HERE – INSTEAD OF ME!'

Richard Halliburton, d.1939

Richard Halliburton was an American adventurer and travel writer best known for swimming the length of the Panama Canal. For his last venture, he commissioned, built and attempted to captain a Chinese junk, the *Sea Dragon*, across the Pacific Ocean from Kowloon to San Francisco, in time for the 1939 Golden Gate International Exposition.

Three weeks into its journey, the *Sea Dragon* ran into a typhoon. Halliburton's cheerful last message, above, was picked up by the nearby SS *President Coolidge*. An extensive search over thousands of miles failed to recover or site any wreckage and Halliburton was assumed, then legally declared, dead seven months later. As a postscript, the skeleton of a Chinese-style boat washed up in San Diego in 1945 and was assumed to be the remains of the *Sea Dragon*.

4

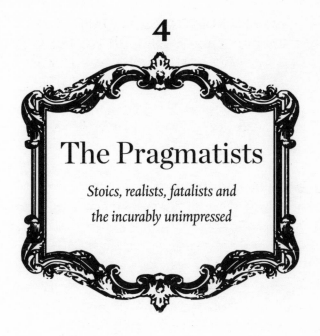

The Pragmatists

*Stoics, realists, fatalists and
the incurably unimpressed*

'BUGGER BOGNOR!'

***

King George V, d.1936

The last words of King George V of England would be glorious, if only they were true. The story long persisted that the king uttered the words on his deathbed. As doctors tried to assure him that he would soon be enjoying the seaside air in Bognor, the sovereign reputedly issued the above exclamation and promptly expired.

In fact, he did say those words, but in a very different context, and several years earlier. Following a lung operation, the king had been persuaded to convalesce in the south coast town, duly packing up the royal family and spending thirteen weeks revivifying by the beach. When, thereafter, his officials suggested the king might want to dignify the town with the accolade 'Regis', the king revealed his true feelings, crying out, 'Bugger Bognor!'

Nonetheless, he relented and Bognor duly became Bognor Regis. The king's actual last words appear more likely to have been 'God damn you!', directed at an unfortunate nurse administering a painful injection.

'I DON'T NEED TO FORGIVE MY ENEMIES – I HAVE HAD THEM ALL SHOT.'

———

Ramón María Narváez, d.1868

Don Ramón María de Narváez y Campos, 1st Duke of Valencia, was a nineteenth-century Spanish soldier and statesman famed for his vigorous suppression of the crown's enemies. Asked by a priest on his death-bed to forgive those who had offended him, his response was chillingly businesslike.

'ON THE CONTRARY!'

———

Henrik Ibsen, d.1906

The Norwegian master dramatist, writer of *Peer Gynt*, *A Doll's House*, *Hedda Gabler* and *An Enemy of the People*, among other staples that revolutionised theatre, is today the most performed playwright in the world after William Shakespeare. Ibsen suffered a stroke in May 1906 and took to his bed. Upon hearing his nurse telling a visitor that his condition was improving, Ibsen spluttered the above correction before dying, one can only imagine to prove his point.

'MY DEAR, BEFORE YOU
KISS ME GOOD-BYE, FIX
YOUR HAIR. IT'S A MESS.'

———

George Kelly, d.1974

O n his deathbed, George Kelly was visited by his niece, who had come to pay her respects to the American dramatist and screenwriter. Kelly, evidently feeling she could have shown a little more respect with regard to her appearance, offered this gentle rebuke.

'MONEY CAN'T BUY LIFE.'

———

Bob Marley, d.1981

Singer, musician, songwriter, populariser of reggae and international symbol of peace and unity, Bob Marley passed away at the tragically young age of thirty-six, victim of a rare type of malignant melanoma. Dying in Miami's Cedars of Lebanon hospital, he spoke the above words to his young son Ziggy, before slipping into unconsciousness.

'I HOPE THE EXIT IS JOYFUL AND HOPE NEVER TO COME BACK.'

Frida Kahlo, d.1954

Mourners at Frida Kahlo's funeral were treated to a decidedly grisly scene. As her open coffin was pushed towards the incinerator doors, a sudden blast of heat made her body sit bolt upright, giving her the look of a grinning banshee with blazing hair, before she disappeared into the flames.

It was one last surprise in a career that thrived on them, including that she survived to become the artist and icon that she did. In many ways, Kahlo's work was coloured by the pain she suffered throughout her life. At the age of eighteen, she was involved in a catastrophic bus accident which left her with appalling injuries, including a broken back, pelvis, collarbone, and ribs, multiple fractures to her legs, a dislocated shoulder, and a ruptured uterus as the result of an iron handrail having pierced her abdomen.

Despite surviving, Kahlo's injuries left her requiring many operations and countless periods of convalescence, as well as with a great deal of pain that would trouble her for the rest of her days. She began painting during her initial three-month recovery from the accident. Since Kahlo was confined by a full-body cast, her mother made her a special easel so that she could paint in bed. Spending long periods alone, Kahlo began to specialise in self-portraits, rationalising, 'I paint myself because I am so often alone and because I am the subject I know best.'

The resulting work was distinctive and highly original, combining traditional Mexican imagery and symbols with dramatic splashes of colour and elements of surrealism. The fame she deserved eluded her in life, probably as a result of her marriage to renowned artist Diego Rivera, whose career overshadowed her own. Rivera was often unfaithful during their turbulent relationship, adding to the stresses and strains of her physical discomfiture. Frida Kahlo died on 13 July 1954, not long after turning forty-seven, and after evincing the above desideratum. Although she didn't allow them to obstruct her, the many pains of her life provided good grounds for her not wanting to return.

'ALL IS STRAW.'

———

Thomas Aquinas, d.1274

Upon receiving a divine visitation, the church father and principal philosopher of the Catholic faith renounced all his works, abandoned his unfinished *Summa Theologiae* – the book which would subsequently underpin centuries of Christian thought – and fell silent for the rest of his days.

'Go on, get out! Last words are for fools who haven't said enough!'

—————

Karl Marx, d.1883

The philosopher, whose writings, including *Das Kapital* and *The Communist Manifesto*, formed the basis for modern international communism, never lived to see the fruits of his labours, though fewer than 100 years after his death half the world would be living under regimes claiming to be 'Marxist'. Marx himself died stateless and penniless in London on 17 March 1883. He shouted this admonition at his housekeeper when she dared to ask if he had any last words.

'WELL, NOW I MUST GO TO MEET GOD AND TRY TO EXPLAIN ALL THOSE MEN I KILLED AT ALAMEIN.'

———

Bernard Montgomery, d.1976

Field Marshal Bernard Montgomery, 1st Viscount Montgomery of Alamein, or simply 'Monty' as he was popularly known, was one of the highest-ranking and most successful British military commanders of World War Two. He was given command of the Eighth Army in north Africa after the initial rout at El Alamein, and defeated the German Army at a second battle there, inflicting upon them their first wartime reverse and forcing them to evacuate north Africa, an action the importance of which cannot be overstated in the history of the war. On his deathbed, the old soldier was haunted by the casualties of his wartime deeds and confessed as much to Sir Denis Hamilton. Hamilton, who served under Montgomery during the war, reassured him, 'Field Marshal, I'm sure they'll be overjoyed to see you.'

'NOW, NOW, MY GOOD MAN, THIS IS NO TIME FOR MAKING ENEMIES.'

———

Voltaire, d.1778

François-Marie Arouet, popularly known by his *nom de plume* Voltaire and one of the most celebrated and versatile of all Enlightenment writers, was throughout his life a fierce critic of the Catholic Church and refused to recant his views at the end of it. As an old man, when he was dying, he was visited by a priest and asked to renounce the devil. Voltaire considered his advice but decided not to follow it, giving the above witty riposte as a reason.

'UTTER NONSENSE!'

Eleanor Roosevelt, d.1962

As Anna Eleanor Roosevelt lay dying, she could reflect on a good and useful life well-lived: as a crusading First Lady to her husband Franklin; as America's first representative to the UN Commission on Human Rights; and as a tireless campaigner on behalf of women and of the disadvantaged throughout the world. What she evidently refused to countenance was the religious musings of a maid who told her she would not die until the reason God had put her on earth was fulfilled, dismissing it with the above superbity.

'LET ME HAVE NONE OF
YOUR POPISH STUFF.
GET AWAY WITH YOU.
GOOD MORNING.'

Thomas Paine, d.1809

Evidently philosopher and author of *The Rights of Man* Thomas Paine was of the same mind as Mrs Roosevelt. Paine, an English-born fomenter of the American Revolution, and a founding father of the United States of America, also had a reputation for making a nuisance of himself by publishing pamphlets attacking pretty much everything and everyone.

Exiled from England for libelling Edmund Burke, he very nearly got himself guillotined in the Terror that followed the French Revolution (it is a mark of his confidence that he got himself elected to the French National Convention despite not speaking a word of French). It was only the somewhat reluctant intervention of future President James Monroe that saw Paine safely repatriated to the United States.

In short, Paine would have been a misfit in anyone's society, and Heaven would have made no exception to that rule. The above chastisement was offered to a priest attempting to officiate at Paine's passing. Only half a dozen people attended Paine's funeral as he had been ostracised for his attacks on Christianity. Paine had left instructions for his body to be buried in a Quaker grave-yard, but he had earlier offended the Quakers so they refused, and he was instead buried beneath a walnut tree.

'IT WASN'T WORTH IT.'

Louis B. Mayer, d.1957

Hollywood movie mogul Louis Mayer had done much in life to look back upon. Born to poor Jewish immigrants from Ukraine, he created and ran Metro-Goldwyn-Mayer (MGM), the leading Hollywood studio during the golden age of film, turning out fifty films a year – among them classics like *Gone with the Wind* – creating countless stars and changing the way America was perceived around the world, through the proliferation of the moving image. None of it was enough for Mayer in the end, though, and as he lay dying with leukaemia in a Los Angeles hospital, he came to the above gloomy conclusion.

'DYING IS A VERY DULL, DREARY
AFFAIR. AND MY ADVICE TO
YOU IS TO HAVE NOTHING
WHATEVER TO DO WITH IT.'

———

W. Somerset Maugham, d.1965

E xcellent advice from the British playwright, novelist
and short story writer, though ultimately difficult to
put into practice. Maugham lived a long and prolific life;
he was born in the year Disraeli became Prime Minister
and died at the age of ninety-one, in 1965, having achieved
sustained critical and popular success for his work that
persists to this day. Despite this, he died a sad, bitter and
lonely man, disenchanted at the corruption of the world
and a prolonged feud with his family.

'I HAVE BEEN ALL THINGS AND IT HAS PROFITED ME NOTHING.'

Septimius Severus, d.211

The founder of the so-called Severan dynasty of Roman emperors, Severus was probably the last half-decent emperor Rome enjoyed before it descended into 100 years of chaos. Essentially a military man, Severus went everywhere and did everything: fighting the requisite wars, pushing the requisite boundaries and consolidating the status quo in existing provinces.

That said, he was a cruel man who enjoyed nothing more than riding his horse over his enemies' naked bodies. However, by far his biggest failing was that he put too much power into the hands of the army. For all their brilliance and versatility, the Romans could never quite grasp basic financial concepts such as inflation and debasement. Under Severus, the Roman denarius was debased drastically as he minted more and more coins to pay the legions. In doing so, he near-fatally undercut the economy and set in train a precedent that would plague Rome until its demise three centuries later.

By investing so much influence in the army, he would ensure the end of civil rule in Rome as the military became the ultimate arbiter of power, deciding who would be made emperor, and who would replace him if he didn't pay well enough. Emblematic of this is Severus's deathbed advice to his son and successor, the disastrous Caracalla, 'Be generous to the soldier, and take no heed of anyone else.'

'I'M BORED WITH IT ALL.'

Winston Churchill, d.1965

Another of life's magnificent overachievers, Winston Churchill was among Britain's finest leaders and was recently voted top in a poll of the country's greatest ever citizens – with a global influence that survives to this day. Towards the end of his life, however, he was beset by ailments and suffered particularly from what he called the 'black dog' of depression. He had a major stroke in 1953 which caused him to retire from his second stint as Prime Minister only two years later. Though he kept his parliamentary seat and tried to remain active in public life, the rigours of a lifetime caught up with him, and with advancing age came numerous strokes and bouts of depression. On 15 January 1965, Churchill suffered another stroke that left him seriously ill. After uttering the above words, he slipped into a coma and died nine days later, aged ninety.

'I WANT NOTHING BUT DEATH.'

Jane Austen, d.1817

Jane Austen is probably the most beloved of all writers in the English language. The four novels published during her lifetime, *Sense and Sensibility*, *Pride and Prejudice*, *Mansfield Park* and *Emma*, along with the posthumous *Northanger Abbey* and *Persuasion*, comprise a canon of literature that is second only to the works of Shakespeare in its influence and popularity. How perverse it seems, then, that her books brought her virtually no fame during her lifetime beyond a few polite reviews.

Austen's death was not a pleasant one, and it was a long time coming – as her final call for release intimates. She began to feel ill more than a year before, beginning a slow and painful physical decline, the symptoms of which are redolent to modern medicine as being possibly Hodgkin's lymphoma or Addison's disease. She struggled on throughout her illness, but in April 1817 was confined to bed, where she died on 18 July, aged just forty-one.

'This is a hell of a way to die.'

George S. Patton, d.1945

Flamboyant, outspoken and permanently toting a trade-mark pair of ivory-handled pistols, General George S. Patton, America's most successful general of World War Two, was not to everyone's tastes, but his death as a result of a car accident just after the war ended came as a terrible shock to all, not least to Patton himself. Patton was paralysed after the crash and the above words were his response to being told that, should he survive, he would never walk again. He died later that night and, in accordance with his wish to be buried with his men, was laid to rest in the Luxembourg American Cemetery.

'EVERY DAMN FOOL THING YOU DO IN THIS LIFE YOU PAY FOR.'

Édith Piaf, d.1963

France's national chanteuse and the world's most distinctive and idolised purveyor of chanson, Édith Piaf left an enduring legacy with autobiographical songs such as 'Non, je ne regrette rien', 'La Vie en rose' and 'Milord'. The product of the liaison of a café singer and circus acrobat, and raised by her brothel-owning grandmother, Piaf came by fortune the hard way, singing her way to fame in the nightclubs of Pigalle. At 4ft 8 in. in height she was nicknamed the Sparrow, and this, her distinctive, plaintive vocal style and her ability to weld her experiences of growing up hard into beautiful songs quickly elevated her to the status of national treasure, despite an ambiguous period during World War Two when she appeared to collaborate with the Nazis. Later on, a series of car accidents followed years of alcohol and drug abuse, which only served to complicate her final illness.

'I HAVE HAD NO REAL
GRATIFICATION OR ENJOYMENT
OF ANY SORT MORE THAN MY
NEIGHBOUR ON THE NEXT
BLOCK WHO IS WORTH
ONLY HALF A MILLION.'

—————

William Henry Vanderbilt, d.1885

This pretty sentiment from the dying businessman,
philanthropist and heir to the Vanderbilt fortune
might come as evidence to some cynics that he simply
hadn't been trying hard enough.

'THERE IS NOTHING PROPER ABOUT WHAT YOU ARE DOING, SOLDIER, BUT DO TRY TO KILL ME PROPERLY.'

———

Cicero, d.43BC

Lawyer, rhetorician and statesman, Marcus Tullius Cicero was one of the leading lights of the Roman Republic in the years before it was subsumed by Augustus and turned into an empire. A waspish man, he was unwise to have made serious enemies during his career, not least among them Julius Caesar's great friend, Mark Anthony, whom he publicly denounced in a series of speeches.

Following the death of Caesar, Mark Anthony went into partnership with Octavian (who would later become Augustus) and had all rivals' and enemies' names noted on a list marking them for death, Cicero among them. Cicero was tracked by soldiers to his villa at Formiae. Rather than resist his fate, Cicero proffered the above words and presented his neck to allow the fatal blow.

Following his death, Cicero's head and hands were cut off and nailed to the Rostra in the Forum, where Mark Anthony's wife pulled out the famous orator's tongue and jabbed repeatedly with a hairpin the organ that had slandered her husband.

'THIS ISN'T *HAMLET*, YOU KNOW. IT'S NOT MEANT TO GO IN MY BLOODY EAR!'

Laurence Olivier, d.1989

The last words of the great Shakespearian actor, spoken to a hapless nurse when she spilled water on him in his hospital bed, are a fitting allusion to the death of the king in the bard's play – poison was poured in his ear whilst he slept.

'Crito, I owe Asclepius a cock. Will you pay him for me?'

Socrates, d.399BC

Dying with his priorities intact, the classical Greek philosopher inveigled upon his friend Crito to settle his earthly debts.

'THE STRONGEST.'

———

Alexander the Great, d.323BC

A sked on his deathbed who he wanted to succeed him, the great military commander replied as above.

'THAT'S SURPRISING, SINCE I HAVE BEEN PRACTISING ALL NIGHT.'

John Philpot Curran, d.1817

John Philpot Curran was an Irish politician, lawyer, judge and wit. Dying of apoplexy, and notwithstanding the discomfort of his condition, Curran remained outwardly jocular to the end. When his physician observed that he coughed with much difficulty, Curran immediately offered the above retort.

'YOU REMEMBER YOUR PROMISE?
YOU WILL DO MY POST-MORTEM?
AND LOOK AT THE INTESTINES
CAREFULLY, FOR I THINK THERE
IS SOMETHING THERE NOW.'

———

Elie Metchnikoff, d.1916

Professional to the last, as he lay dying the Russian bacteriologist began to record the progress of his illness in a diary, to wit, 'After several crises of tachycardia, following upon a slight grippe with asthma, I had congestion of one lung with pleuritic exudate. Though some improvement followed after that, nevertheless I am tormented by fits of sweating followed by cough and oppressive shivering.' Eventually he became obsessed with discovering the cause of his own certain demise, speculating diagnoses and, in his last words, importing a colleague to perform the confirming post-mortem, even though Metchnikoff himself could not benefit from the knowledge.

'OBEY THE LAW OF MOSES, REMAIN UNITED AND ALWAYS CONSULT YOUR MOTHER. OBSERVE THESE THREE POINTS AND YOU WILL SOON BE RICH AMONG THE RICHEST AND THE WORLD WILL BELONG TO YOU.'

―――――

Mayer Amschel Rothschild, d.1812

With this advice to his five sons, Mayer Rothschild, founder of the Rothschild banking dynasty, went the way of all flesh. His sons must have listened to his words of wisdom, for they went on to establish banks in London, Paris, Vienna, Naples and Frankfurt, amassing the largest private fortune anywhere in the world.

'PUT THAT BLOODY
CIGARETTE OUT!'

———

Saki, d.1916

Hector Hugh Munro, better known by the *nom de plume* Saki, was a British short story writer who special-ised in witty sketches and satires on Edwardian society. Aged forty-three at the outbreak of the First World War, he was officially too old to enlist, but he refused a com-mission and joined the 2nd King Edward's Horse as an ordinary trooper. Sheltering in a bomb crater during the Battle of the Ancre, Munro spotted a fellow soldier lighting a cigarette. Realising the glow would give enemy snipers something to aim at, he issued the above admo-nition. However, it was too late and Munro himself was shot through the head, dying instantly.

'I AM SORRY TO TROUBLE YOU,
CHAPS. I DON'T KNOW HOW YOU
GET ALONG SO FAST WITH THE
TRAFFIC ON THE ROADS
THESE DAYS.'

———

Ian Fleming, d.1964

The James Bond creator, a heavy smoker throughout his life, suffered a heart attack whilst dining with friends at a Canterbury hotel. Perhaps typically, for the man who created the quintessential English character, Fleming's last words were an apology to the ambulance crew who collected him for the inconvenience he was causing.

'I AM ABOUT TO – OR AM GOING TO – DIE: EITHER EXPRESSION IS CORRECT.'

Dominique Bouhours, d.1702

Practical to the last, the seventeenth-century French grammarian and philologist Dominique Bouhours used his dying words to perfect even the grammatical expression of mortality.

'I'M A FUCKING DOCTOR!'

———

R. D. Laing, d.1989

Ronald Laing was a Scottish psychiatrist who specialised in the study of mental illness. He suffered a coronary during a game of tennis, drawing a crowd of concerned onlookers to his side. When someone called out for a doctor, Laing himself replied with this somewhat unhelpful response.

'I'D RATHER BE SKIING THAN DOING WHAT I'M DOING.'

———

Stan Laurel, d.1965

A s half of one of the most celebrated comedy double acts of all time, English actor Stan Laurel made over 100 films, later being honoured with a Lifetime Achievement Academy Award for his pioneering work in comedy, as well as a star on Hollywood Boulevard's Walk of Fame.

Days after suffering a heart attack, the ailing Laurel told his nurse he wouldn't mind going skiing right now. When she replied she didn't know he was a skier, he replied he wasn't, he would just rather be skiing than dying.

'I AM JUST GOING OUTSIDE.
I MAY BE SOME TIME.'

Captain Lawrence Oates, d.1912

Captain Lawrence Edward Grace 'Titus' Oates was a member of Robert Scott's *Terra Nova* Expedition to Antarctica between 1910 and 1913. Having been pipped to the South Pole by Roald Amundsen's rival expedition, Scott's team ran headlong into trouble on the return journey. Extremely adverse weather conditions, dwindling food supplies, injuries and the onset of frostbite meant that their hopes of reaching salvation at a pre-laid food depot looked slight.

Oates, whose feet had become severely frostbitten, realised he was slowing his colleagues down and thus compromising their chances of survival. Scott recorded in his diary of 16 March how Oates said the above words and walked out of the tent, into a blizzard and to his certain death.

His name has since become a byword for self-sacrifice. Tragically, however, although his comrades struggled on, they too succumbed to the weather and fatigue, dying nine days after Oates, and only eleven miles from safety.

'THE WAR IS AT ITS HEIGHT – WEAR MY ARMOUR AND BEAT MY WAR DRUMS. DO NOT ANNOUNCE MY DEATH.'

Yi Sun-sin, d.1598

General Yi Sun-sin was a brilliant Korean naval commander who battled the invading Japanese in the Imjin War of the Joseon Dynasty. Defeating a superior Japanese force at Sachon in December 1598, Yi Sun-sin gave orders to pursue the fleeing enemy. During the chase, however, he was mortally wounded by a stray arquebus bullet from an enemy ship.

Sensing the battle was still in the balance, and not wishing his troops to be demoralised by the loss of their popular leader, Yi Sun-sin issued this dying command. Hiding the body, Yi Sun-sin's nephew Yi Wan donned his uncle's armour and led the unknowing Koreans to victory.

5

The Visionaries

*Mystics, thinkers, legends and
the downright inspirational*

'WOMEN MUST TRY TO DO THINGS
AS MEN HAVE TRIED. WHEN THEY
FAIL, THEIR FAILURE MUST BE BUT
A CHALLENGE TO OTHERS.'

Amelia Earhart, disappeared 1937

A pioneering female aviator and the first woman to fly solo across the Atlantic Ocean, among other extraordinary feats, Amelia Earhart was a true inspiration. Her childhood was troubled, to say the least, yet she pulled herself through it by sheer strength of ambition, keeping a scrapbook of newspaper clippings about women who had succeeded in male-dominated fields, determined not to lose out in life simply because of her gender. In 1937, she embarked on her most ambitious challenge to date – an attempt to fly around the world. It was to be her last.

After having completed nearly 30,000 miles of her journey, and with only 7,000 miles remaining, Earhart and navigator Fred Noonan set off in her twin-engine Lockheed Electra on 2 June for the tiny Howland Island in the mid-Pacific. Flying into very cloudy weather, it was hard to navigate and Earhart sought bearings from the US Coast Guard cutter *Itasca*, stationed off Howland Island. Intermittent transmission followed but was interrupted by static. Her final transmission to the *Itasca*, as she was still desperately trying to ascertain her bearings, was, 'We are running north and south.' The ship heard nothing more and, despite an extensive air and sea search covering 250,000 square miles of ocean, Earhart's fate remains a mystery.

Before departing on her final trip, she left a letter with her husband to be opened in the event of her death. She wrote: 'Please know I am quite aware of the hazards. I want to do it because I want to do it. Women must try to do things as men have tried. When they fail, their failure must be but a challenge to others.'

'STANDING, AS I DO, IN THE VIEW
OF GOD AND ETERNITY, I REALISE
THAT PATRIOTISM IS NOT ENOUGH.
I MUST HAVE NO HATRED OR
BITTERNESS TOWARDS ANYONE.'

———

Edith Cavell, d.1915

Edith Cavell was a British nurse working in German-occupied Brussels during the First World War. Whilst treating wounded soldiers from both sides of the conflict, she also arranged for nearly 200 Allied soldiers to escape from Belgium, for which activity she was arrested by the Germans and accused of spying. On 12 October 1915, despite calls for clemency, Cavell was shot at dawn by a German firing squad.

The execution caused worldwide condemnation. Sir Arthur Conan Doyle captured the feeling of the time when he wrote, 'Everybody must feel disgusted at the barbarous actions of the German soldiery in murdering this great and glorious specimen of womanhood.' In fact, Cavell's death happened at a time when the war had been going badly for the Allies, and proved a major recruiting call, with volunteers swelling the ranks for the British Army.

The night before her execution, Cavell gave a statement including the above words to an Anglican chaplain who had been allowed to see her. The same words are now inscribed in a statue of Edith Cavell in London's St Martin's Place, just off Trafalgar Square.

'I KNOW YOU ARE HERE TO KILL ME. SHOOT, COWARD, YOU ARE ONLY GOING TO KILL A MAN.'

———

Che Guevara, d.1967

The face of Ernesto 'Che' Guevara de la Serna stares out from the walls of student bedrooms across the world. With his smouldering good looks, his advocacy of armed revolution and a penchant for vintage motorcycles, Che fulfils the romantic ideal of the revolutionary.

Hailing from a middle-class Buenos Aires family, the young Guevara spent years travelling around South and Central America, becoming increasingly convinced that the solution for the poverty and inequality he witnessed there lay in violent uprising. He was given the opportunity to test his hypothesis when he played a central role in Fidel Castro's guerrilla war against Cuba's Batista regime. After occupying several key roles in Castro's government, and helping to secure the amity and assistance of Soviet Russia, Guevara fell out with his fellow revolutionaries, who were piqued at his popularity with the masses.

He announced his desire to spread revolution throughout the developing world and set off for Africa, then Bolivia. It was in the latter, whilst leading rebel forces against the government of René Barrientos Ortuño, that Guevara met his end.

Tipped off by a local informant, the Bolivian Army encircled Guevara's camp, and he was wounded and captured in the ensuing firefight. He was taken to the village of La Higuera, where, two days later, Barrientos gave the order to execute him. As his killer entered the room, Guevara delivered the above imperative, and the order was carried through. Buried without ceremony in a secret location, in 1997 Guevara's remains were discovered, exhumed and returned to Cuba where he received a state funeral.

'YOU WILL NOT FIND ME ALIVE AT SUNRISE.'

Nostradamus, d.1566

As spoken to his departing secretary, Jean de Chavigny, the purported final words of the sixteenth-century French alchemist and mystic Michel de Nostredame were as accurate a prophecy as any he might have made. De Chavigny returned the next morning to find his master quite deceased.

'I HAVE OFFENDED GOD
AND MANKIND BECAUSE MY WORK
DID NOT REACH THE QUALITY
IT SHOULD HAVE.'

———

Leonardo da Vinci, d.1519

The final words of the Italian painter, sculptor, architect, inventor, scientist and musician are a little harsh.
Alright, he might have left the Mona Lisa's eyebrows off,
but her smile is to die for.

'THAT WAS A GREAT GAME OF GOLF, FELLERS.'

Bing Crosby, d.1977

The last day of American singer and actor Bing Crosby's life was, at least, a good one. Taking a break from a concert tour of Britain, Crosby flew to Spain to indulge his passion for golf. He and his golf partner played a leisurely game around the course, stopping only for photographs and a genial rendition of 'Strangers in the Night' for some star-struck construction workers labouring nearby. Crosby lost the game but only by a stroke and, as they strolled back towards the clubhouse, he said the above words before collapsing and dying from a massive heart attack.

'I AM NOT GOING.
DO WITH ME WHAT YOU LIKE.
COME ON! COME ON!
TAKE ACTION! LET'S GO.'

Chief Sitting Bull, d.1890

Sitting Bull was the Native American chief and holy man who united the Sioux tribes in their struggle against the United States for the American Great Plains. The discovery of gold in the Black Hills of South Dakota led to conflict between the native Sioux and the federal authorities, a conflict that would blossom into the Indian Wars of the 1870s and would itself be a part of America's attempts to address the problem of exactly what to do with its indigenous peoples. The answer, as it so depressingly often is, was to subdue and displace them.

Not that Sitting Bull and his people would go quietly. His finest hour came when he and Crazy Horse led a confederation of tribes to an astonishing victory against General Custer's troops at the Battle of the Little Bighorn in 1876, wiping out an entire US Army cavalry battalion and plunging 'civilised' white America into a state of shock. In practical terms, however, the victory was to be short-lived; a few months later, his people starving, Chief Sitting Bull surrendered to US forces and was finally forced to settle on a reservation.

Years later, after a stint working in Buffalo Bill's Wild West show, Sitting Bull returned to the reservation and his tribe, intending to peacefully live out the rest of his days. However, he was wrongly perceived by US Indian Agent James McLaughlin to be an instigator of a potentially insurrectionist religious movement, the Ghost Dance, and orders were drawn up for Sitting Bull's arrest. Police from nearby Fort Yates surrounded Sitting Bull's house and forcibly brought him and his wife outside. Chief Sitting Bull said the above words in protest, upon which a Lakota brave pulled up his rifle and wounded the arresting officer, who himself discharged a pistol into Sitting Bull's chest. Another policeman then shot Sitting Bull in the head and, in the fight that followed, six policemen and eight Sioux were killed, including Sitting Bull himself.

'IT WAS THE FOOD! DON'T TOUCH THE FOOD!'

Richard Harris, d.2002

After the veteran Irish actor finished filming the Harry Potter series, he took ill and retired to a suite in London's Savoy Hotel. In fact, he was battling lymphatic cancer and, concerned at his worsening condition, his sons went to the hotel and kicked his room door in. Finding their father emaciated and weak, they called an ambulance. As he was being wheeled through the hotel lobby, he sat up on his stretcher and shouted the above words to the startled guests.

'SURPRISE ME.'

Bob Hope, d.2003

The great American entertainer died of pneumonia two months after his 100th birthday. On Hope's deathbed, his wife asked him where he wanted to be buried, to which Hope replied, 'Surprise me.' In fact, he was interred in the Bob Hope Memorial Garden at San Fernando Mission Cemetery in Los Angeles.

'I AM DYING. PLEASE… BRING ME A TOOTHPICK.'

Alfred Jarry, d.1907

French symbolist writer and proto-Surrealist Alfred Jarry made a living from confounding the ordinary. Jarry wore a loaded revolver on his meanderings around Paris (Picasso, who idolised him, acquired it after Jarry's death and did much the same). When his neighbour protested at Jarry's shooting at targets in his own apartment, fearing that he might harm her children, he helpfully responded, 'If that should ever happen, Madame, we should ourselves be happy to get new ones with you.' The undisputed master of the absurd, it should come as no surprise that, dying of tuberculosis aggravated by the consumption of ether and drugs, his last request was itself profoundly unconventional.

'DOES NOBODY UNDERSTAND?'

James Joyce, d.1941

The Irish novelist is generally recognised as one of the most important writers of the twentieth century, with works such as *Dubliners* and *A Portrait of the Artist as a Young Man*, but particularly *Ulysses*, leaving a profound legacy to both literature and academia.

Joyce died on 13 January 1941, following botched surgery for a perforated ulcer. Slipping in and out of consciousness before finally passing away, his last words are reported to have been the above plea for comprehension from the medical staff treating him.

However, literary wags have found it amusing to speculate that Joyce was referring to the complexity of his own later work *Finnegans Wake*, which, with its linguistic experimentation, free association of ideas and stream of consciousness narrative, has been described as the most difficult work of fiction in the English language to actually read.

'AS TO ME, I LEAVE HERE TOMORROW FOR AN UNKNOWN DESTINATION.'

Ambrose Bierce, d. circa 1914

In 1913 and at the age of seventy-one, the American critic, journalist and short story writer Ambrose Bierce went to Mexico to report on the revolution taking place in that turbulent land. In Ciudad Juárez he linked up with the army of Pancho Villa and observed the Battle of Tierra Blanca, before departing with Villa's troops for Chihuahua. Nothing is known of Bierce's whereabouts thereafter.

His last known communication is a letter he sent to his friend Blanche Partington on 26 December, including the above statement. US authorities in Mexico launched an official investigation, even interviewing some of Villa's men, but despite this and the independent enquiries of Bierce's friends, nothing is known of his fate. Local legend persisted that Bierce was executed by firing squad in the town churchyard but this has never been substantiated, and has been dismissed by some historians as improbable.

Indeed, it is even disputed whether Bierce made it to Mexico – there is some question as to the legitimacy of the letter to Partington. What became of Ambrose Bierce, despite a multitude of theories, seems likely to remain a mystery for ever.

'ONLY ONE MAN EVER UNDERSTOOD ME. AND HE DIDN'T UNDERSTAND ME.'

Georg Wilhelm Hegel, d.1831

The German Enlightenment philosopher Georg Wilhelm Hegel said this of his former student Johann Philipp Gabler, and it expresses perfectly the sheer impossibility of knowing anyone, even oneself. Or something like that.

'SO, THIS IS DEATH. WELL!'

———

Thomas Carlyle, d.1881

The nineteenth century's pre-eminent essayist and social commentator was somewhat unimpressed by the experience of dying and made his thoughts typically plain.

'TELL THEM I'VE HAD A WONDERFUL LIFE.'

Ludwig Wittgenstein, d.1951

One of the twentieth century's most original and influential thinkers, Wittgenstein was not known for his cheery character. He once revealed that he wanted to write a philosophical treatise entirely on jokes, but had dismissed the idea as impractical on the grounds that he lacked any sense of humour whatsoever. When his last words were repeated by the doctor he had told them to, people who knew Wittgenstein were surprised that he even had the capacity to enjoy his life.

'IT IS TIME NOW TO END THE
GREAT ANXIETY OF THE ROMANS,
WHO HAVE GROWN WEARY IN
WAITING FOR THE DEATH OF
A HATED OLD MAN.'

Hannibal, d.181BC

Hannibal, one of the great commanders of antiquity and perhaps the finest military strategist of all time, invaded Italy at the start of the second Punic War and occupied Rome's back yard for fifteen years, decisively trouncing her legions at Trebia, Trasimene and Cannae. After a time, Rome changed her tactics and sent Scipio Africanus to invade Hannibal's native Carthage, drawing the latter back to north Africa and defeat at Scipio's hands. There followed a period of exile, with Hannibal again fighting Rome, but this time as a mercenary for other great powers. Eventually, betrayed to the Romans by one of his own paymasters, Hannibal drank poison, leaving behind a letter declaring the above.

'Damn it! How will I ever get out of this labyrinth?'

Simón Bolívar, d.1830

The resplendent Simón Bolívar y Palacios, El Liber-tador, was industrious even by the standards of the nineteenth century, when exceptional statesmen were perhaps more prevalent. Having freed his native Vene-zuela from the yoke of Spanish colonialism, he did not rest until he had forged a chain of independent sovereign states across the South American continent, creating a union that incorporated Ecuador, Peru, Colombia, Pan-ama, Venezuela and, finally, Bolivia – where the grateful natives named the country after him.

As is so often the case with magnificent overachievers, his days ended unhappily in bitterness and disappoint-ment. People eventually tired of him, accusing him of betraying his original republican ideals, and when he cast down the mantle of command the entire continent dissolved into sporadic bouts of civil war. Perhaps predict-ably, Bolívar had opened the door to the curiously Latin

American phenomenon known as *caudillismo*, whereby a series of charismatic strong men would replace each other in coup after bloody coup.

Pathetically, he died surrounded by luggage in a room in Cartagena, waiting to set sail for Europe and self-exile. His last words have been interpreted as a nod to the ultimate failure of his dream of union. However, the sheer scale of his achievements and the short space of time in which he made them (he died at the age of only forty-seven) is dizzying, and the reverence in which he is held today across the continent he liberated is a fitting testament to an extraordinary individual.

'THIS IS FUNNY!'

Doc Holliday, d.1887

As Doc Holliday lay dying of tuberculosis in a Colorado hotel room in November 1887, he chanced to look down the bed at his unshod feet. The veteran of nine gunfights remarked that it was hard to credit he was dying without his boots on, having assumed, along with those who knew him or simply read about his exploits, that he would eventually be gunned down as so many adventurers on the western frontier had been before him.

In fact, John Henry 'Doc' Holliday began his career, somewhat incongruously, as a dentist, only moving to the south-west in the hope that its arid climate might ease the symptoms of his consumption. Once there, his awareness of the finite mortality afforded him by a rapacious illness lent him a recklessness that would secure a reputation as one of the west's most fearless gunfighters, a reputation that was cemented by his role as Wyatt Earp's deputy in the famous gunfight at the OK Corral.

'WHAT HAS HAPPENED TO ME?'

Elisabeth, Empress of Austria, d.1898

The terrible fate of Elisabeth, Empress of Austria, Queen of Hungary and Queen Consort of Croatia and Bohemia, was compounded by two otherwise innocuous personal traits. Firstly, she was a fiercely independent woman, often travelling alone incognito and eschewing the monotonous mechanisms of security usually detailed to personages of her rank. Secondly, she was obsessed with her figure, investing a great deal of time on her wardrobe and spending hours being sewn into her corsets and copious undergarments.

Neither of these facets were failings in and of themselves, but they did lend a hand to the fatal consequences arising from an assassination attempt in Geneva in September 1898. In the early afternoon, she and a lady-in-waiting set out for a walk down the promenade on Lake Geneva. There she was attacked by Italian anarchist Luigi Lucheni, who had recognised the thinly disguised empress and seized his opportunity to strike. Lucheni stabbed Elisabeth once above the left breast with a four-inch stiletto blade before fleeing.

All happened so quickly that Elisabeth hadn't time to take in what had befallen her. In the time it then took bystanders to remove the empress's clothes and corsets, pulling off yards of silken underclothing and unwrapping the poor woman like a mummy, she had suffered an irrevocable loss of blood. She slipped into unconsciousness and died.

'Dear me! I think I'm turning into a god...'

Vespasian, d.79

Vespasian, founder of the Flavian dynasty, enjoyed an unusual distinction for a Roman emperor in that he died at an advanced age and of natural causes. Subdued by illness in Aquae Cutiliae, Vespasian delivered the above quip on the fact that dead emperors were generally deified according to Roman custom, then, trying to raise himself, expired in the hands of his slaves.

'IT'S ALL BEEN
RATHER LOVELY.'

_____

John le Mesurier, d.1983

Actor John le Mesurier is best known to English audiences for his role as Sergeant Arthur Wilson in the BBC sit-com *Dad's Army*, though he featured in countless films and TV roles across a wide-ranging career. Despite or possibly because of his tendency to play supporting or minor roles, le Mesurier was extremely popular during his lifetime, embraced by a loving public and elevated to the status of national treasure. One explanation for his popularity might lie in his relaxed attitude to his art. He invariably played 'a decent chap all at sea in a chaotic world not of his own making'. On his deathbed he was able to look back on a life well-lived and offer the above reflection.

'Say good-bye to Pat, say good-bye to Jack and say good-bye to yourself, because you're a nice guy.'

Marilyn Monroe, d.1962

The last recorded words of troubled movie star Marilyn Monroe were spoken to English Rat Pack actor Peter Lawford on the evening of 4 August 1962. Lawford had called earlier in the day to invite Marilyn to dinner but Marilyn had refused. Something about Monroe's tone made Lawford uneasy and he called again later to check up on her. Monroe, who was by this time deeply dependent on drugs and alcohol, dismissed him with the above line.

'Pat' refers to Lawford's wife, Patricia Kennedy, and 'Jack' is her brother, the President of the United States, with whom Monroe had a brief but obsessive affair earlier that year. Lawford tried calling back but the line was engaged. Increasingly concerned, he had his business partner telephone Monroe's attorney, who in turn contacted Monroe's housekeeper.

Accounts of the timeline of her death are conflicted, but she was found dead in the bedroom of her Los Angeles home by psychiatrist Dr Ralph Greenson in the early hours of 5 August. She had her telephone in her right hand and a pill bottle lay empty on her nightstand.

'IT HAS ALL BEEN VERY INTERESTING.'

———

Lady Mary Wortley Montagu, d.1762

Aristocrat, poet and letter writer, Lady Mary Wortley Montagu is chiefly remembered today for her correspondence sent whilst travelling round the Ottoman Empire as wife to the British ambassador to Turkey, for her pioneering social observations and her successful campaign for the introduction of smallpox vaccination in eighteenth-century England.

Lady Mary made her way around Europe, often in service to the crown, and her letters back today provide an unrivalled eye onto the history of her time. Her parting words, laced with typically English understatement, deliberately fail to encompass the observations and experiences of a gloriously diverse life.

'OF COURSE I KNOW WHO YOU ARE. YOU'RE MY GIRL. I LOVE YOU.'

_____

John Wayne, d.1979

Marion Robert Morrison was the archetype of rugged American manhood – at least he was after he adopted the stage name John Wayne. Towards the end of his life, his nomenclature reduced even further and he was referred to simply as 'The Duke'.

The Duke dominated the movie world for more than three decades. Mostly starring in westerns, he was an American icon who seemed to transcend the physical realm, becoming the very embodiment of the pioneer spirit the young nation identified itself with.

Dying of stomach cancer and passing in and out of consciousness, the Duke awoke to find his daughter's hand in his. She asked if he knew who she was, to which he replied with the above words, before again becoming unconscious and passing away.

Wayne had wanted a Spanish epitaph engraved on his grave, '_Feo, Fuerte y Formal_', translating as 'Ugly, Strong and Dignified'. However, his headstone actually bears a line from an interview he gave to *Playboy* magazine, 'Tomorrow is the most important thing in life. Comes into us at midnight very clean. It's perfect when it arrives and it puts itself in our hands. It hopes we've learned something from yesterday.'

'NOW COMES THE MYSTERY!'

Henry Ward Beecher, d.1887

Henry Ward Beecher was a celebrated liberal-minded Congregationalist preacher and abolitionist whose posthumous fame is somewhat obscured by that of his sister, the novelist Harriet Beecher Stowe, and was somewhat tarnished in his own lifetime by his involvement in an adultery scandal. Ultimately, however, the latter did not diminish his congregation's love for him and, upon his death, New York announced a city-wide day of mourning. Struck down by a stroke on 8 March 1887, before he died Beecher made the above exclamation.